Images of Oklahoma

IMAGES OF OKLAHOMA

A pictorial history

with text by Bob L. Blackburn

Oklahoma Historical Society
Oklahoma City, Oklahoma

Library of Congress Catalog No.: 84-61286
Published 1984. Second Printing 1990

Blackburn, Bob L.
Images of Oklahoma: A Pictorial History

1. Oklahoma: Photographic History. 2. U.S. History—West: Photographic History. 1. Title.

ISBN 0-941498-36-0 (cloth)

Table of Contents

Preface

Oklahoma is a land of contrast and beauty, a unique state with a blending of many cultures. This historic diversity, from nomadic hunters to urban pioneers, is the subject of *Images of Oklahoma*.

This is not intended to be a complete history of Oklahoma; rather, it is a selective picture story of ordinary people and their efforts to survive, prosper, and enjoy life. Their story is seen here through the lens of a camera.

The genesis of this book was the Image Photographic Exhibit, assembled as an integral part of the Oklahoma Image Project. Funded by a federal grant from the National Endowment for the Humanities and administered through the Oklahoma Department of Libraries, the Image Project emphasized humanities programming through libraries.

Photographs were collected from archives, such as the Western History Collections (University of Oklahoma Library) and the Oklahoma Historical Society, and contests were held in various communities to uncover photographs owned by families and businesses. The result was a compilation of more than 500 historic images that revealed the diversity of everyday life in Oklahoma.

The photographs were enlarged, mounted, and assembled into a portable exhibit that was made available for public programming. From April of 1980 to October of 1981 the exhibit was viewed at 32 locations in 28 communities in Oklahoma, becoming the most popular accomplishment of the entire project.

Several members of the Oklahoma Legislature, led by David Riggs of Tulsa, realized that the photographs in the exhibit offered a unique view of our state's history. To keep the photographs in circulation, they funded this book and assigned editorial production and publication to the Oklahoma Historical Society and the Oklahoma Department of Libraries.

The first task was to purchase prints of the photographs, a process that took more than six months. They were arranged topically and, where possible, chronologically. A chapter breakdown had been established by the Image Project committee, but due to the characteristics of the book format, this organization was altered slightly.

A greater challenge was the poor quality of many photographs, which had not been a problem for the public exhibit. For the book, contrast, clarity, and detail became critical considerations. We replaced several photographs with better images and eliminated a few that would not reproduce at all. To enhance all of the pictures, we used a tri-tone printing process that used black, red, and yellow ink to hold the maximum detail in each reproduction.

The editorial design of the book was in large part determined by the interpretive importance of the photographs. To provide historical background, we used short narratives written with a "broad brush" to capture the essence of each historical topic. That text, placed at the beginning of each chapter, was followed by photographic images that provided the texture of "how it really was." Captions were used primarily as simple identification. We hope the combination will promote interest in Oklahoma history and encourage further reading and research.

This book was made possible through the efforts of many individuals. Dr. Anne Hodges Morgan, the planning director and first administrator of the Image Project, directed the early stages of collection. Jack Haley, Assistant Curator at the Western History Collections, used his vast knowledge of Oklahoma history to narrow the selection process.

The project and book were consistently supported by leadership and staff at the Oklahoma Department of Libraries, including Robert L. Clark, Jr., Director; Howard Lowell, Administrator, Oklahoma Resources Branch; and Jan Blakely, Head, Publications Division.

At the Oklahoma Historical Society, staff time for writing and completing the ambitious project was arranged by C. Earle Metcalf, Executive Director. Staff members who worked on the book and ensured the quality of production were art director, Bob Cornish, who handled all design, layout, and art work; assistant editor, Gordon Moore, who organized files and established initial production and editorial schedules; and office manager, Linda Ward-Taremi, who provided administrative support throughout the project.

Special thanks go to three historians who read the manuscript and offered editorial and conceptual suggestions: Louis Coleman, Deputy Executive Director at the Oklahoma Historical Society; Odie B. Faulk, professor of history at Northeastern Oklahoma State University; and A.M. Gibson, professor of history at the University of Oklahoma.

Without the help of these people, this book would not be available to the public.

Finally, I want to thank my father, Bob L. Blackburn, Sr., a retired trooper with the Oklahoma Highway Patrol and a retired professor of history. He supported my education, encouraged my writing, and sparked my interest in the rich history of Oklahoma. To him, I dedicate this book.

Images of Oklahoma

Land
of the Red Man

In the Choctaw language, Oklahoma means "red people." It is a fitting tribute, for today more than 60 tribes are represented in the population of the state. Their accomplishments, their traditions, their leadership are important threads in the tapestry of our cultural heritage.

The first nomadic wanderers entered Oklahoma about 18,000 B.C. Hunters and gatherers, they lived off the land, gradually developing complex social structures, efficient hunting techniques, and eventually, cultivation of the soil. By 1541, when the first Europeans entered Oklahoma, the Indians of the region had experienced transcontinental trade, highly developed artwork, and organized religion.

From the sixteenth to the nineteenth centuries, the Indians of Oklahoma were swept forward by the winds of change. The horse, acquired from the earliest Spaniards, improved their ability to hunt buffalo. Trade, fueled by the European demand for furs and horses, provided the Indians with metal tools and firearms.

Ironically, the sources of these material advances—Europeans and Americans— destroyed the Indians' isolation. Confronted by an expanding American nation, Oklahoma became an island of Indian survival—one vast reservation known as the Indian Territory.

Although bent by the forces of acculturation, the Indians were rooted in the traditions of their forefathers, creating a unique blending of two cultures. Shoulder to shoulder appeared bark huts and frame houses, mocassins and neckties, gourd ladles and iron kettles.

By the late nineteenth century, when photographers entered the territory, the Indians of Oklahoma offered a unique cultural portrait unmatched anywhere in the world. It was a society rich in variety and contrast, laying the ground work for the survival of traditional Indian culture in Oklahoma.

Cheyenne Lance Society.

Log cabins, tipis, and brush covered arbor on the Gafte Family Ranch—signs of a multi-cultural society.

Stately mansion of Seminole Governor John F. Brown, located near Sasakwa.

Kaw bark hut photographed in 1880 (top right).

Pawnee mud lodge (middle right).

Traditional summer arbor built by Good Eye, a Kiowa and mother of Jim Apeatone (bottom right).

INDIANS MUD LODGE

Ponca Squaw Dance, one of the many ceremonies which survived the acculturation efforts of the reservation era (top left).

Frame and bark roofed summer house, built by Sac and Fox Indians about 1889 (middle left).

Winter camp of Mow-way, or Hand Shaker, a Comanche head man who led his band during the trauma of acculturation (bottom left).

Cheyenne-Arapaho camp near Fort Reno, 1890 (top right).

Howling Knight, a Cheyenne seen here in front of his tipi in 1910 (bottom right).

7

8

Creek women, dressed in Anglo clothing and making sofka, a fermented corn dish (top left).

Cheyenne woman, wife of Black Horse, leading a traditional dog travois (top center).

Pawnee women, in front of a tent and tipi covered with agency-supplied canvas, scraping a hide as their mothers and grandmothers had done (bottom left).

Apache woman carrying firewood (top right).

Reflecting traditional methods of dressing buffalo meat at the site of a kill, a band of Indians near Anadarko skin and butcher a steer (bottom right).

Five headmen, representing the Comanche, Cheyenne, and Kiowa tribes, are seen here in traditional dress in a 1900 model Buick.

Chiefs.

Voting for the Principal Chief of the Seminole Nation. Each candidate's supporters lined up on respective sides of the street (top right).

Choctaw lighthorsemen, in 1893, represented a unique blending of traditional law ways and Anglo-American institutions of law enforcement (bottom right).

Voting

12

For Home
and Honor

Military service for many Oklahomans has been a gripping experience, a bittersweet mixture of adventure and sacrifice. Through the smoke of their battles, the epic proportions of our history unfold—a roster of duty, courage, and sometimes, death.

The first soldiers entered the region to explore the land and make peace with Indians. In their wake dragoons came to establish forts and posts, such as Gibson and Washita, where they found a hard, lonely, thankless life filled with difficulty and danger. Poorly supplied and decimated by disease, they nonetheless did their best in maintaining peace between warring tribes and between Indians and settlers.

The Civil War pitted brother against brother, neighbor against neighbor as the war between the states engulfed the land of the Five Civilized Tribes. Indian armies, both Union and Confederate, fought a series of bitterly contested battles that left many on the field of action. One of the last Confederate forces to surrender in 1865 was an Indian regiment led by Cherokee General Stand Watie.

For the next thirty years cavalry and infantry operated from Fort Sill, Fort Reno, Camp Supply, and other outposts. They tracked and battled elusive plains Indians, chased and arrested horse thieves and bootleggers, and found and drove out the persistent boomer armies of David L. Payne. Through their efforts, they prepared the territory for peaceful settlement.

Since then, Oklahomans in the armed services have cut a wide swath through history. During the Spanish-American war, they were the pride of the Rough Riders, a band of cowboys and frontier youth led by the dynamic Theodore Roosevelt. In successive wars, from World War I to the war in Viet Nam, Oklahomans have responded to the call of duty.

Through the ranks of the Army, Navy, Air Force, Marines, Coast Guard, and National Guard, soldiers from Oklahoma have established an enviable record of service in peace and war. Their legacy, of duty written in the blood of battle, is the pillar that supports our freedom.

U.S. Army officers assigned to Guthrie during the land run of 1889. Captain Arthur MacArthur is on the left.

14

Army camp located at the site where Fort Reno would be built (top left).

Fort Reno, founded in 1875, looking northeast (middle left).

Troops camped on Cottonwood Creek just outside Guthrie, 1889 (bottom left).

Indian scouts of Troop C, 5th Cavalry, Fort Reno, 1890 (top right).

Military parade at Fort Reno, 1890 (middle right).

Soldiers at Fort Sill gathered around their chaplain, Father Isidore Ricklin (center), 1891 (bottom right).

Ruins of Fort Gibson barracks, circa 1900, a physical legacy of the military in Oklahoma (top left).

Fort Washita ruins, circa 1960, all that was left of the post established in 1843 (top left center).

Cavalry inspection at Fort Supply, an outpost founded in 1868 as a supply base for troops under the command of George Armstrong Custer (middle left).

16

Confederate Home at Ardmore, established in 1907 as a hospital and retirement home for Confederate veterans *(bottom left)*.

Captains Allyn K. Capron *(left)* and Robert H. Bruce, Oklahomans who served in the Rough Riders. Capron was killed leading a cavalry charge up San Juan Hill *(top right center)*.

Oklahoma National Guardsmen, circa 1915 *(top right)*.

Review at Camp Frank Canton, 1909 *(bottom right)*.

17

Firing 3" Field Gun at

More than 4,000 Woodward County citizens gathered to see recruits off to boot camp during World War I (top left).

Just a few of the Indian soldiers who served in uniform during World War I (middle left).

Target practice with field gun at Fort Sill, 1917 (bottom left).

Cemetery of the unknown dead at Fort Gibson (top right).

Ruins of Fort Gibson barracks, circa 1920 (middle right).

U.S.S. Oklahoma at Berehaven, Ireland, while it was attached to the Atlantic Fleet between 1919 and 1921 (bottom right).

Brigadier General Raymond S. McLain, a native of Oklahoma City, was commander of the 90th Infantry Division that had just taken a French village during World War II *(top right)*.

Captain Raymond S. McLain at Fort Sill during World War I *(middle right)*.

General Patrick Hurley, a native Oklahoman, with Mao Tse-tung, Lin Tze-han, General Chu Teh, and Chou En-lai during World War II *(bottom right)*.

Officers and men of the U.S.S. Tulsa, docked in Hong Kong, 1981 *(top left)*.

Workers at Tinker Air Force Base maintained three eight-hour shifts a day during World War II *(middle left)*.

Scrap metal drive in Altus, 1942 *(bottom left)*.

CATTLE

Ranch
and Range

Cowboys, horses, and longhorn cattle—these are images of the Old West that linger in the hearts and minds of the public. To most people these images come from movies and dime novels. To Oklahomans, they are part of our heritage, a chapter in the settling of this land we call home.

Even the pre-Columbian Indians of the region had their concept of cattle—the buffalo, or American bison. Roaming in vast herds across the plains and wooded hills of the Southwest, the buffalo was a "commissary on hoof," an undomesticated source of meat, clothing, and tools.

Citizens of the Five Civilized Tribes were among the first pioneers to bring cattle into the Indian Territory. By 1878 more than 55,000 citizens of the Five Tribes owned cattle. One of them, C.W. Turner, an adopted member of the Creek Nation, ran a herd exceeding 5,000 head. Even the Indians of the plains tribes developed herds. Quanah Parker, a Comanche leader, owned 500 head by the 1880s.

The most popular images of cattle in Oklahoma focus on the great cattle drives— rivers of longhorn beef pushed north by range-tough cowboys. Four primary trails cut across Oklahoma from Texas to the railheads in Kansas: the East Shawnee Trail, the West Shawnee Trail, the Chisholm Trail, and the Western, or Dodge City Trail.

Even before this era ended, ranchers were carving spreads from the ocean of grass and running thousands of head of cattle in the territory. After 1889 and the land openings to non-Indian settlement, the range cattle industry retreated before scientific herd improvement, fenced pasturage, and smaller, mixed operations.

A common element throughout this era of ranch and range was the cowboy, a unique blend of horseman, handyman, and animal doctor. From trail driving and branding mavericks to building fence and baling hay, the cowboy cut a wide swath through Oklahoma's frontier heritage.

The images of the cowboy and his world are enduring, representing a challenging life of tending cattle, raising families, and battling the elements in a promising new land.

23

Dipping cattle, one of the cowboys' many jobs.

Buffalo, or American Bison, the Indians' "commissary on hoof." (top left).

Headquarters of the "U" Ranch, a 150,000 acre spread in the Cherokee Outlet founded by Major Andrew Drumm in 1870 (bottom left).

Cowboys, cattle, and grass—an image of courage and independence on the unbroken prairies of western Oklahoma (top right).

Herds of cattle stretching as far as the eye could see were common sights before homesteaders settled the land (middle right).

Cowboys of the CC Ranch eating a little breakfast during roundup (bottom right).

Horses, saddles, lariats, spurs, and wide brim hats—the tools of the cowboys' trade (top left & center).

Branding pen at the Townsend and Pickett Ranch (bottom left).

Branding on the open range (top right).

Branding calves at the annual roundup was the only means of identifying stock on the open range (middle right).

With chuck wagon and Sibley tents for their only comfort, cowboys stop for lunch at a buffalo wallow (bottom right).

Mr. and Mrs. J.A. Selman visiting a cow camp in Woodward County, a rich area of grassland on the western edge of the Cherokee Strip (top left).

Herding cattle through the streets of Seiling, a town in Dewey County (bottom left).

Cowboys and cattle in a grove of trees on the Townsend and Pickett Ranch (top right).

Indian cowboys, a sign of cultural adaptation in Indian Territory (middle right).

Stockyards, where cattle were loaded onto railroad cars for shipment to market (bottom right).

Towns_____ __ ___ R____ __ Cow Boys. D17

Stock Yards Canadian City, Tex.

OKLAHOMA

CAPT. PAYNE'S
OKLAHOMA COLONY

Will move to and settle the Public Lands in the Indian Territory before the first day of December, 1880. Arrangements have been made with Railroads for

LOW RATES.

14,000,000 acres of the finest Agricultural and Grazing Lands in the world open for

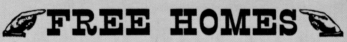 FREE HOMES

For the people—these are the last desirable public lands remaining for settlement.

Situated between the 34th and 38th degrees of latitude, at the foot of Washita Mountains, we have the finest climate in the world, an abundance of water, timber and stone. Springs gush from every hill. The grass is green the year round. No flies or mosquitoes.

The Best Stock Country on Earth.

The Government purchased these lands from the Indians in 1866. Hon. J. O. Broadhead, Judges Jno. M. Krum and J. W. Phillips were appointed a committee by the citizens of St. Louis, and their legal opinion asked regarding the right of settlement, and they, after a thorough research, report the lands subject under the existing laws to Homestead and Pre-emption settlement.

Some three thousand have already joined the colony and will soon move in a body to Oklahoma, taking with them Saw Mills, Printing Presses, and all things required to build up a prosperous community. Schools and churches will be at once established. The Colony has laid off a city on the North Fork of the Canadian River, which will be the Capital of the State. In less than twelve months the railroads that are now built to the Territory line will reach Oklahoma City. Other towns and cities will spring up, and there was never such an opportunity offered to enterprising men.

MINERALS!

Copper and Lead are known to exist in large quantities—the same vein that is worked at Joplin Mines runs through the Territory to the Washita Mountains, and it will be found to be the richest lead and copper district in the Union. The Washita Mountains are known to contain **Gold and Silver**. The Indians have brought in fine specimens to the Forts, but they have never allowed the white men to prospect them. Parties that have attempted it have never returned.

In the early spring a prospecting party will organize to go into these Mountains, and it is believed they will be found rich in GOLD AND SILVER, Lead and Copper.

The winters are short and never severe, and will not interfere with the operations of the Colony. Farm work commences here early in February, and it is best that we should get on the grounds as early as possible, as the winter can be spent in building, opening lands and preparing for spring.

For full information and circulars and the time of starting, rates, &c., address,

T. D. CRADDOCK,
General Manager,
Wichita, Kan.

GEO. M. JACKSON,
General Agent,
508 Chestnut St., St. Louis.

October 23d, 1880.

"Go Forth and Possess the Promised Land"

On April 22, 1889, 50,000 people gathered along the borders of the Unassigned Lands, anxious to claim a piece of the Promised Land. At high noon the signal sounded and the race began—on horseback, in buggies, in wagons, and on trains the wall of landseekers surged forward. By nightfall virtually every part and parcel of the territory was claimed.

This dramatic scene, reproduced in countless books and movies, was only one chapter in the settlement of Oklahoma Territory. Preceding the run was the boomer movement, a ragtag army of landseekers led by David L. Payne and William Couch demanding that the federal government open unassigned Indian lands to settlement. After a series of daring boomer raids and an effective propaganda campaign in newspapers and in Congress, the land was opened.

Following the run of 1889 came a series of land openings, each providing another piece in the jigsaw puzzle that would become Oklahoma Territory. In 1890 the Panhandle, known as No Man's Land, was added to the territory by congressional action. Then in 1891 the Iowa, Sac and Fox, Shawnee, and Pottawatomie lands were opened by run. A year later the Cheyenne-Arapaho reservation was dissolved and surplus land opened.

In 1893 the largest of the openings took place—the run into the Cherokee Outlet, which attracted more than 100,000 people. Many of them settled in towns such as Perry, Enid, and Woodward; others scattered across the rich prairie. During the next eight years other large tracts were added to Oklahoma Territory, including the Kickapoo lands, old Greer County, the Kiowa-Comanche and Wichita-Caddo lands, and the Big Pasture.

Claiming the land, however, was only part of the battle. Next came the challenge of breaking the soil, taming the elements, and surviving the solitude of homesteading. Despite the odds, the fight would be won, adding another unique chapter to the history of Oklahoma.

Boomer poster, a sign of coming change in the heart of Indian Territory.

Last boomer camp of David L. Payne, seen here at the left holding an axe (top left).

Scene from the movie, "Cimarron," recreating the run of 1889. Unfortunately, no historic photographs survived (middle left).

Guthrie as it appeared on the afternoon of April 22, 1889. The frame building is the U.S. Land Office (bottom left).

First train bound for Perry from the southern border of the Cherokee Strip on September 16, 1893 (top right).

Thousands of landseekers lined the streets of El Reno during the lottery of 1901 (middle right).

El Reno train station, passageway for settlers hoping to get a piece of land in the 1901 opening (bottom right).

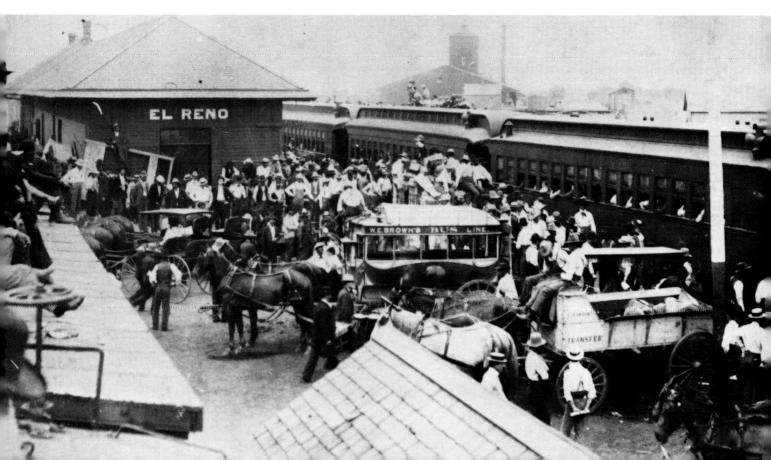

After the land runs, most families lived in tents until better shelter could be built (top left).

Black homesteaders near Guthrie, sharing the dream of a new beginning in a new land (bottom left).

Homesteaders in the Kiowa-Comanche lands *(top right)*.

Sod houses, livestock, family, and hope—signs of success on the Oklahoma frontier *(bottom right)*.

Land of the Fair God

Restless migration was the initial act in the drama of Oklahoma. But still the land was untamed, a wilderness of prairie and forest that offered a new chance for America's farmers. The legacy of their conquest, of roots set deep in the soil, is the bedrock upon which our society is built.

Cultivation began among the Indians of Oklahoma about 900 A.D. Growing beans, corn, and pumpkins, thereby decreasing their reliance on migratory hunting, they established semi-permanent villages which fostered more complex social structure, art, and commerce.

Citizens of the Five Civilized Tribes brought a long tradition of agriculture with them across the Trail of Tears. While most practiced subsistence farming, growing only what they could eat or barter, a few mixed-bloods grew extensive cash crops. In the 1850s, Colonel Robert M. Jones, a Choctaw slave owner, cultivated more than 5,000 acres of rich bottom land, much of it in cotton.

Cotton also was king in Oklahoma Territory after the land openings, for it held the greatest promise of cash return. A man with 40 acres, a mule, and a large family could successfully cultivate and harvest cotton, then expect a return of $25 to $50 an acre in good years.

Wheat was another important crop in the territories. After suffering severe drouth from 1889 to 1896, Oklahoma farmers looked to wheat as the best dry land crop, able to mature with as little as 20 inches of annual rainfall. In 1897, when the price of wheat rose from 48 cents to 76 cents a bushel, the farmers of Oklahoma planted 1.5 million acres of the crop.

Despite drouth, low prices, boll weevils, high transportation costs, and over-production, the farmers of Oklahoma persevered. And as they prospered, the towns and cities of the territory grew. Built upon a base of agricultural productivity, the economy of Oklahoma steadily improved, providing the capital for industry, oil, and commerce.

Virtually all Oklahomans can trace their family heritage directly to the land, usually within a single generation. The values learned from tilling the soil—hard work, optimism, and persistence—have made a lasting imprint on the people of the state.

37

Ester Orr sterilizing milk crocks by sunning them on her farm in the Johnson Community near Shawnee, circa 1910.

Dugouts, constructed from sod bricks, served many farm families in the Cherokee Outlet, 1894 (top left).

Makeshift frontier dwelling that combined soddy, dug-out, and half timber construction in western Oklahoma, 1890 (middle left).

Well groomed log cabin that belonged to a prosperous farmer, his affluence reflected in the glass windows, wood shingles, and fine clothes (bottom left).

Frame houses were built after the bumper crops of 1897 and 1898 (top right).

Windolph homestead, in Ellis County, located in the western reaches of the old Cherokee Strip (middle right).

Well's farm, near Tonkawa, situated farther east near the Crosstimbers (bottom center).

Hogs and hog pens, signs of investment and potential cash on the Windolph homestead (bottom right).

Fremont Bowen, a pioneer farmer who broke the thick prairie sod on his claim four miles northeast of Coyle (top left).

A plowing demonstration near Sentinel. Horses and mules would remain the primary sources of power on Oklahoma farms until WW I (middle left).

Steam powered tractor, seen here in 1901 near Hobart, belonged to Russell Polson (bottom left).

Vineyards on the I.C. Renfro experimental station near Sulphur. By 1900 fruit and wine production were important sources of cash to territorial farmers (top right).

Corn was grown for food and fodder, but was not a major cash crop, 1912 (middle right).

Cutting kafir corn near El Reno in the 1920s (bottom right).

Harvest at the Chilocco Indian School, near the Kansas border in the old Cherokee Outlet (top left).

Stacking hay on the 101 Ranch, one of the largest farming operations in the territory (middle left).

Hauling broomcorn to market in the Oklahoma Panhandle, 1910 (bottom left).

Steam-powered wheat threshing machinery, a major reason for agricultural productivity on the high plains, 1899 (top right).

Men and women picking strawberries near Guthrie (middle right).

C.W. Cole ranch near Altus, where workers are putting feed into the silo, 1912 (bottom right).

43

Making sorghum syrup in the southeastern counties of the former Indian Territory, where cane was cultivated (top left).
Cotton gin at Sentinel (bottom left).

Cotton bales ready for shipment to market, 1915 (top right).

Streets of Elk City, crowded with men ready for the buying and selling of the cotton harvest, 1907 (bottom right).

TRANSPORTATION

From Here
to There

Oklahoma has always been a land of open spaces, where getting from "here to there" has posed a challenge. From Indians and explorers to farmers and merchants, every man and woman has faced the limitations of transportation.

The first transportation in Oklahoma was walking. Nomadic Indians, carrying simple possessions on their backs, followed migratory game across the land. Periodically, they used water craft and dog-powered travois, but walking continued to be the primary alternative until the 1600s.

The first transportation revolution followed the arrival of the horse. With mounts for hunting and raiding, Indians became "lords of the Southern Plains." Europeans, with knowledge of the animal's potential, used their horses to conquer the New World.

Explorers, trappers, and traders also relied on waterways for transportation. Rafts, canoes, and river boats were efficient means of moving men and materiel, but the rivers of Oklahoma proved to be unreliable and often dangerous.

Roads for land travel were built, first by the military for access to forts and posts, then by the territorial government for trade and postal delivery. Unfortunately, travel by horse, wagon, and stage was slow and inefficient, limiting the economic development of the land.

The solution was the railroad, ribbons of steel that first entered Oklahoma in 1871. Desperately sought by merchants, farmers, and town promoters, a network of rail quickly spread across the territory. By 1910 most counties in the state were served by a railroad, opening the land to development and trade.

During the twentieth century travel was further improved by motorized vehicles such as automobiles, trucks, and aircraft. Using roads, airports, and waterways built by city, county, state, and federal governments, these adaptable vehicles ushered in a new transportation revolution.

From horses to jets, transportation has altered the lives of all Oklahomans. Settlement patterns, cultural development, and economic prosperity—all have been affected by transportation and man's efforts to get "from here to there."

47

Car trouble on an early Oklahoma road.

Steamer "City of Muskogee"
at Wharf Muskogee Okla, July 20, 1908.

Photo by Pierson.

Stern-wheeler river boat, docked at Muskogee on the Arkansas River, 1908 (top left).

Doan's Crossing on the Red River, a low water landmark where horsemen and wagon trains forded the unpredictable stream (bottom left).

Courting buggy (top right).

Stage station on the Guthrie to Kingfisher stage line, June of 1889. (bottom right).

Stage Station bet' Guthrie & Kingfisher June 4th

267

49

Building a railroad bridge north of Camargo in Dewey County (top left).

Santa Fe railroad gang laying track through Tonkawa, 1899 (bottom left).

Santa Fe Depot, a unique structure that reflected the promise of early Shawnee (top right).

Electric streetcar on the Guthrie Railway Company line, circa 1910 (bottom right).

51

Oklahoma highway construction began slowly in the 1910s, then boomed in the 1920s with federal aid and state supervision (top left).

Metz automobile and a steel truss bridge, signs of progress in overland transportation (middle left).

Wilson & Co. delivery truck. Such vehicles improved the efficiency and profitability of hauling goods to market (bottom left).

Indian motorcycle and its proud owner, Scott Carne, of Blue Jacket, Oklahoma (top right).

Airplanes were a fascination by the 1910s and a revolutionary method of transportation by the 1920s (bottom right).

54

The Bounty of the Land

While farmers and merchants built homes and towns upon the land, miners, drillers, and lumberjacks harvested the bounty of the good earth. To those pioneers, the natural resources of Oklahoma represented an essential foundation of economic strength, veins of wealth that fueled prosperity and fired the engines of industry.

Prehistoric nomads relied upon the earth's bounty for their very survival. They used natural wildlife and plantlife for food, clothing, and weapons, and even harvested minerals for tools and trade. Salt, deposited in river beds by flooding torrents, was brushed from grasses with turkey feathers. Flint, found in isolated pockets, was mined and shaped into arrow points.

Mixed-blood citizens of the Five Civilized Tribes also exploited natural resources. They opened salt works, harvested timber, and hunted fur-bearing animals. They made baskets from cane, pottery from clay, and dyes from walnuts, sassafras, and wild onions. The most profitable industry in Indian Territory, however, was coal mining.

From earliest settlement, shallow deposits of coal were tapped for home use. Then, in 1871, intermarried Choctaw, J.J. McAlester, opened the first commercial coal mine in the Choctaw Nation. By 1907 the mines of Indian Territory employed more than 8,000 workers and produced 3 million tons of coal each year.

In 1891, in the northeast corner of Indian Territory, the empire of coal was challenged when extensive deposits of lead and zinc were discovered near Peoria. Towns swelled and prospectors spread across the land. One mine located near Quapaw produced more than $1 million in ore during a 20-year period.

Other important natural resources in the history of Oklahoma included timber, gold, gypsum, glass sand, salt, clay, iodine, stone, helium, and dolomite. The impact of this wealth, both in human and material terms, changed the course of history and added to the physical and cultural heritage of our state.

55

Lead and zinc prospectors using a cable tool rig to search for ore deposits near Vinita, 1904.

Coal miners working a strip pit near Chelsea, 1922 (top left).

Deep shaft miners working for the Lucky Kid Mining Company (bottom left).

Coal miners, recruited mainly from Southern Europe, swelled the non-Indian population of Indian Territory, 1890s (top right).

Miners of the Henryetta Coal Company with a mule-drawn coal car (bottom right).

Top works and steel tipple at the Milby and Dow mine #9, 1914 *(top left)*.

Coal cars, laden with ore, surface from the Milby and Dow mine #5 to be weighed, 1914 *(top center)*.

Oklahoma Coal Company mine #2 near Henryetta, with cord wood to fire the steam engine boilers *(bottom left)*.

Anxious crowd around the mouth of the Bolen Mine, located near McAlester, after a mine explosion and cave in, December 17, 1929 (top right).

Steam powered shovel used to remove overburden and coal from strip pits (bottom right).

Lead and zinc shaft miners in the Tri-State Mining District near Miami, 1906 (top left).

The mine and plant of the Picher Lead Company, 1920 (middle left).

Underground operations of a lead and zinc mine in the Miami District in Ottawa County, circa 1910 (bottom left).

Top works of a gold mine shaft located near Snyder. In 1904 one geologist claimed that there were 2,500 gold mines in the Wichitas (top right).

Gold Bells M&M stamping mill, a massive 50-ton ore-reduction cyanide plant built a mile south of Wildman in 1904 (bottom right).

Granite works operated by the Pellow Brothers near Granite (top left).

Primitive salt works in Greer County, 1897 (middle left).

Salt factory in Blaine County, which pumped brine through boiling vats to extract the salt, 1898 (top right).

Ore washing operation, probably for glass sand, located south of Davis, 1910 (middle right).

Oklahoma Portland Cement Company plant in Ada, built about 1910, secured limestone from a quarry about seven miles south of town (bottom).

Harvesting timber with axes and cross-cut saw *(top left)*.

Early Oklahoma City saw mill, powered by a steam tractor, 1889 *(middle left)*.

P.B. Wilson Lumber Yard in Okemah, 1910 *(bottom left)*.

Small "peckerwood," or portable saw mill, in the piney woods of Atoka County, circa 1895 *(top center)*.

Walnut logs, harvested primarily from the Creek Nation, were sent to Germany where they were used to make gun stocks, 1901 *(top right)*.

Log train unloading a harvest into the mill pond near Moyers, 1916 (middle right).

James Brown Lumber Company in Anadarko, 1902 (bottom right).

A Sea
of Black Gold

They were pioneers from Oklahoma's oil frontier—
drillers, rig builders, pipe layers, and lease hounds—men and women who created an empire, a way of life that was unique in the American experience. Together they found the oil and gas that fueled the fires of progress.

The first oil deposits in Oklahoma were discovered in 1859 by Lewis Ross, a mixed-blood Cherokee. The driller did not pay much attention, however, for he was drilling for salt water. To him oil was a nuisance, a black liquid that had few applications and little value.

With demand for petroleum increasing and delays of tribal regulation fading with allotment, drillers eventually returned to the territory. In 1901 the first commercially successful oil well in Oklahoma was drilled near Red Fork, a small town southwest of Tulsa. Although the well produced only 10 barrels a day, it attracted an army of wildcatters and investors, each confident that he or she would find a sea of black gold.

Four years later, on a lease about 12 miles south of Tulsa, Robert Galbreath and Frank Chesley struck oil and gas at 1,400 feet. To their delight the well flowed more than 600 barrels a day; more importantly, the discovery opened the Glenn Pool oil field and ignited a frenzied rush to the oil fields of Oklahoma.

For the next thirty years oilmen brought in a series of unprecedented oil discoveries—the Greater Osage, the Cushing, the Healdton, the Three Sands, the Greater Seminole, and the Oklahoma City fields. Each generated increased drilling and production activity and each kept Oklahoma at the top of oil producing states. From 1901 to 1935 Oklahoma wells flowed almost 4 billion barrels of oil worth more than $5 billion.

Since that golden age of exploration, the oilmen of Oklahoma have continued their search for petroleum. In the off-shore depths of Lake Texoma, in the stripper wells of old fields, and in the deep sands of the Anadarko Basin, drillers are still searching for and finding oil and gas. Their legacy—of gambling adventure, investment, and economic productivity—is an important and colorful epoch of Oklahoma's past.

Cable tool operators, with the driller next to the telegraph wheel and the roughneck on the floor of the derrick.

Teamsters delivering pipe from Hatfield, Arkansas, to a pipeline project in eastern Oklahoma (top left).

Hauling oil field equipment across the Cimarron River near Drumright, 1914 (bottom left).

Steam boiler, used to generate power for a cable-tool rig, being pulled off a railroad car in Yale (top right).

Yale, a boom town in the center of the Cushing oil field, 1914 (middle right).

Drilling machinery, ready for the trip to the oil patch, 1906 (bottom right).

First Oklahoma Geological Field Survey party, seen here near Watonga in 1900. Left to right are Paul J. White, Roy Hadsell, and Charles Gould (top left).

Survey crew members recording geological formations in the Arbuckle Mountains. Later oilmen would use their notes and maps to find underground oil deposits (middle left).

Portable pulling mast, used to erect cable tool rigs, near Dewey, 1908 (bottom left).

Oil gusher, located north of Yale, circa 1914 (top center).

Venting the natural gas after the cable tool rig has been dismantled (top right).

Cable tool derrick under construction, 1913 (bottom right).

Pipeline workers connecting pipe in the Glenn Pool oil field *(top left)*.

Forest of closely spaced derricks, a common sight before the first conservation efforts of the 1930s *(middle left)*.

Increased wholesale and retail distribution of petroleum products, seen here in Chelsea during the 1920s, encouraged exploration and production *(bottom)*.

Hauling pipe for the Sinclair Oil Company in the Seminole Field, 1927 (top right).

Pipe was shipped into the oil fields by rail, then hauled to the site by truck or mule team (middle right).

73

Bartlesville, Ind. Ty. - Drum.

74

9

Cable tool rigs (top left).

Derricks near Bartlesville, one of the oil boom towns which survived and prospered, 1906 (middle left).

Road between Oilton and Cushing, 1915 (bottom left).

Rotary rig, with drill stem that would be used as the hole was drilled deeper (top center).

Derrick floor of a rotary rig (middle right).

Quay Oil Field, opened in Payne County in 1914 (bottom right).

Wooden derrick, reportedly toppled by high winds (top left).

Oil tanks burning in the Three Sands oil field, circa 1925 *(bottom left)*.

The big fire at Drumright, August 28, 1914 *(top right)*.

Cannons were used to blow holes in the sides of burning oil tanks, allowing crude to escape *(bottom right)*.

Matson Oil Company boarding house in the Osage field, 1905 *(top left)*.

Home in the oil patch, with well paid worker, his wife, and their prized possessions *(bottom left)*.

Company housing in the Jennings oil field *(top right)*.

Cleveland, Oklahoma, with derricks and houses side-by-side, circa 1905 *(bottom right)*.

Early rotary rigs with wooden derricks (top left).

Cable tool rigs, surrounded by stacked pipe and make-shift housing (middle left).

Three Sands, an oil boom town which prospered during the early 1920s (bottom left).

Main Street of Seminole, an occasional swamp of mud and stalled vehicles, 1926 (top right).

Due in part to overproduction of oil, gasoline was selling for 11 cents a gallon in the 1930s (bottom right).

Modern day rig hands working on the floor of a rotary derrick *(top left)*.

Geologist inspecting core samples at Stigler, 1967 *(top center)*.

Offshore oil well, drilled in 1947 in the Gulf of Mexico *(bottom left)*.

Kerr-McGee refinery in Cushing, 1954 *(top right)*.

Gas plant at Wynnewood, 1955 *(bottom center)*.

Natural gas storage facilities *(bottom right)*.

The Forgotten Frontier

Every Oklahoman, whether raised in the city or in the country, has memories of small towns on a Saturday morning. Hair cuts, cokes at the drug store, farmers market, shopping for a new pair of shoes—these are the images of Main Street.

The earliest villages in Indian Territory were merely wide places in the road, usually a few buildings crowded around a military fort, trading post, or Indian agency. Towns such as Park Hill, Skullyville, Doaksville, Eagletown, and Boggy Depot surfaced across the territory like islands in the ocean.

The first full-service cities, founded after 1871, followed railroad construction into the territory. The earliest were towns such as Wagoner, Muskogee, and Durant, established along the tracks of the MKT. As other rail lines penetrated the Indian lands, towns such as Ardmore, Sapulpa, and Purcell arose from the unbroken soil.

On April 22, 1889, the urban frontier exploded overnight as land-hungry pioneers rushed for town lots in Guthrie, Edmond, Oklahoma City, Norman, and Kingfisher. In the span of a few hours thousands of homeseekers congregated in each prairie oasis.

As other tracts of land were opened to non-Indian settlement, towns such as Perry, Woodward, Watonga, and Lawton were organized. Then, with statehood and agricultural prosperity, hundreds of small towns appeared throughout the countryside. Some survived; others, bypassed by railroads, withered and died.

Although each town was unique, there were similarities. Most were located on rail lines and led by boosters who described their hometowns as the center of the world. Each attracted doctors, lawyers, land developers, journalists, and preachers. Each offered the paying public hay and feed stores, dry goods stores, drug stores, hardware stores, and saloons.

Oklahoma's urban frontier held forth opportunity to individuals willing to start life again in a new land. The lessons learned during those early years—self-government, free enterprise, and civic promotion—would provide the young state with a vast pool of experience and talent, qualities that would be needed in coming decades.

85

Main Street in Tulsa, circa 1907.

Perry, the largest city in the Cherokee Strip (Outlet), October 3, 1893 (top left).

Townsite of Anadarko, where lots were being sold in August of 1901 (middle).

Guthrie, on April 27, 1889, five days after the land run (bottom left).

Courthouse under canvas, represented by these court officials in the early days of Anadarko's settlement, 1901 (top right).

Oklahoma City, viewed from Grand (Sheridan Ave.) and the Santa Fe tracks only weeks after the run of April 22, 1889 (bottom right).

Main St. Lisbon Ok. June 4th

88

Main Street of Kingfisher, June 4, 1889 (top left).

Orlando, a small town in the northeastern corner of the Unassigned Lands (middle left).

Ripley, Oklahoma Territory, with utility poles and gazebo as signs of progress (bottom left).

Ponca City, with the community well and water supply in the middle of Main Street, 1897 (top right).

Streets of Oklahoma City, where a generation of two and three story brick buildings replaced the first frame structures by 1900 (bottom right).

89

Inauguration of Territorial Governor Frank Frantz, held on the steps of the Carnegie Library in Guthrie, January 15, 1906 (top left).

Railroad depot at Fairfax, lifeline for community survival (bottom left).

Main Street of Sentinel, a typical small town in 1910 with a few brick commercial buildings and a scattering of houses (top right).

Market day in Chelsea, a town located on the Frisco tracks in the old Cherokee Nation (bottom right).

SANTA FÉ DEPOT FAIRFAX, OKLA.

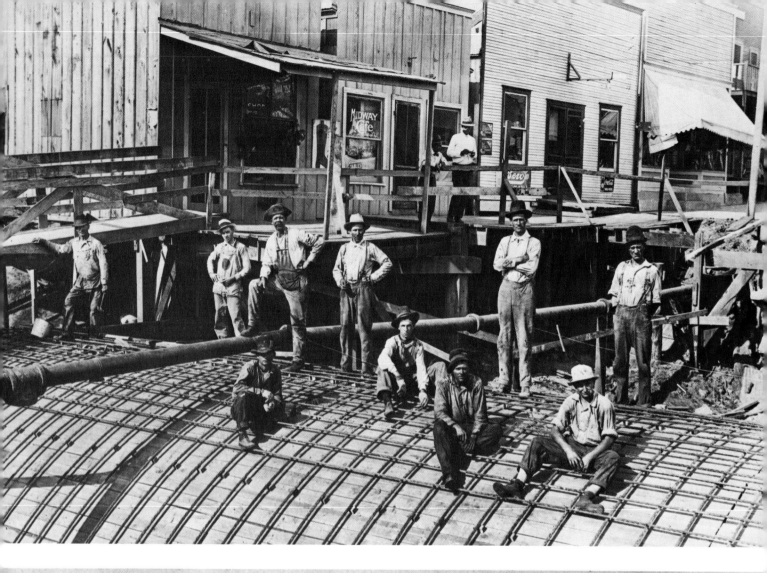

First Water Works of Perry Martin Bro's Proh. Ockrath

Bridge construction on Main Street in Drumright, 1919 (top left).

First water works in Perry, built by the Martin Brothers in October of 1893 (bottom left).

Horse-drawn firetruck, probably with volunteer firefighters, in Frederick, 1907 (top right).

Ardmore Police Department, 1915 (bottom right).

Freedom
of the Market Place

From the dawn of settlement in Oklahoma, merchants established trading posts and stores where Indians and pioneers could purchase basic supplies. This tradition of the free market place, where supply followed demand, created a vibrant economic foundation that encouraged personal initiative and material investment.

Prehistoric Indians in the region were the first traders on the landscape. Packing goods as diverse as sea shells and salt, these Native American merchants established well defined trade routes and traveled as far as the Gulf of Mexico and the Mississippi River valley.

Europeans came to the future state primarily for trade. Indians bartered pelts and horses to French adventurers for tools and merchandise. Reaping the benefits of their bargaining skills, the Wichitas built fortified villages and traded with both white men and nomadic Comanches.

Many settlements in the territory grew around frontier trading posts established by pioneers such as Jesse Chisholm, a mixed-blood Cherokee, and Abel Warren, an American from Connecticut. These daring frontiersmen built active centers of commerce in the heart of Indian land.

After the Civil War, towns spread across the territory and merchants led the charge. Attracted by potential profits in an undeveloped land, they built dry goods stores, drug stores, hardware stores, and feed stores. Shoulder to shoulder with these retail pioneers came butchers, bakers, launderers, and harness makers. Together, they provided the food and fiber for sustained growth.

In the best traditions of free enterprise and personal initiative, the early day merchants of Oklahoma saw opportunity and acted. Their contributions to economic development, to the quality of life, and to the growth of towns were important building blocks in settling the land.

King's Kash Grocery, located in Roosevelt, 1927.

96

Traders store at Wellston, Indian Territory, a community located in the future Lincoln County (top left).

"Shorty" Fenno's 16-mule team wagon, which hauled freight between western Oklahoma towns from 1900 to 1907 (middle left).

Horse traders, who traveled from town to town in the territory, in their campground near Idabel, 1904 (bottom left).

Turkeys brought to town for the T.H. Fariss Meat Market in Taloga, 1910 (top right).

Coffee, bacon, flour, and molasses were just a few of the items that could be purchased at the Cyclone Grocery store in Anadarko, 1901 (bottom right).

THE CYCLONE GROCERY D.F. DILLON PRO.
BARRETT. N.W. COR SQ.

W.H. Butcher butcher shop in Oklahoma City, 1901 (top left).

Baker in El Reno preparing bread for crowds gathered for the land opening of 1901 (bottom left).

Killingsworth General Store at Tidmore, 1905 (top right).

98

Grocery store in Washita County, complete with canned goods, pastries, cracker barrel, and post office *(middle right)*.

Lilly General Store in Elk City, well stocked and decorated at Christmas time *(bottom right)*.

99

H.B. Campbell's Hay and Grain store, with scales to weigh wagons loaded with feed. *(top left)*.

J.M. Hamilton's feed store and livery in Tonkawa, called the "Star Barn," where horses and buggies could be rented or boarded *(bottom left)*.

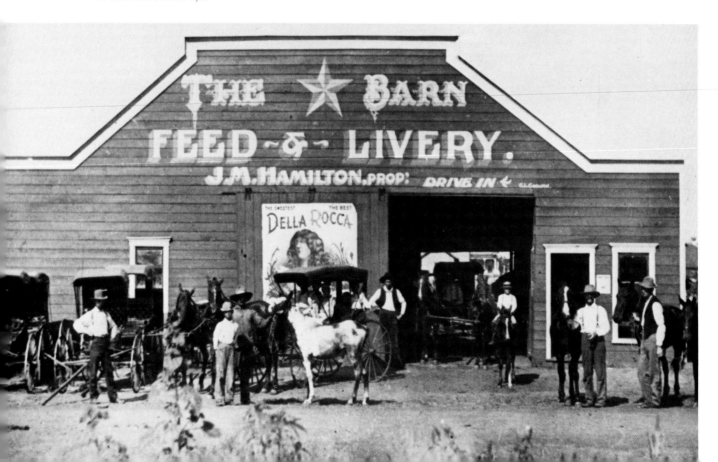

Carnegie Drug Store, located in the former Wichita-Caddo reservation, was a social center and gathering place, 1903 (top right).

General merchandise store and saddle shop, a sign of economic progress in Woodward (bottom right).

102

Owl Drug Store, the first drug store in Carnegie, was founded in 1901 by A.C. Fitschen of Hobart (top left).

Dr. E.B. Hamilton's drugstore was a popular place for afternoon refreshment in Wilburton, 1905 (top right).

Palace Pharmacy and Drug Store in Wilburton, 1898 (bottom left).

Kingfisher drug store, decorated with mounted animals and birds (bottom right).

103

Outdoor hardware store in Guthrie, April 30, 1889, only eight days after the land run *(top)*.

First National Bank of Duncan, organized in 1893, and the A.M. March Hardware Store, 1894 *(middle left)*.

Anadarko in 1901, a boom town with merchants offering their wares from tents *(bottom left)*.

Merchants of Hobart, proudly displaying McCormick reapers in 1903 (middle right).

Wooden buildings, each with the typical territorial store front, lined the Main Street of Hollis in 1903 (bottom right).

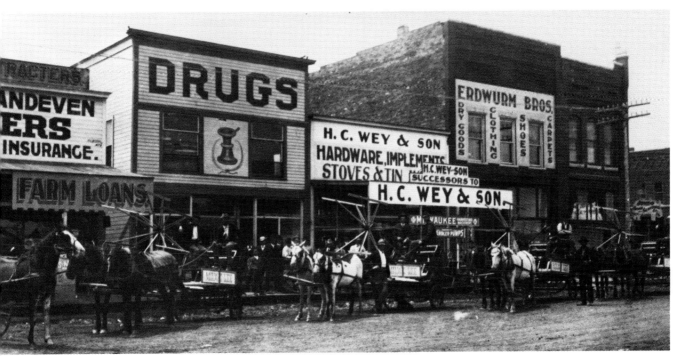

Levite's Handy Corner Store, located in Apache, 1915 *(top left)*.

Dry goods store in Duncan, with wearing apparel from hat pins to corsets, circa 1900 *(bottom left)*.

Department store in Wynnewood, 1900 *(top right)*.

Lowenstein's Department Store in Apache, 1908 *(bottom right)*.

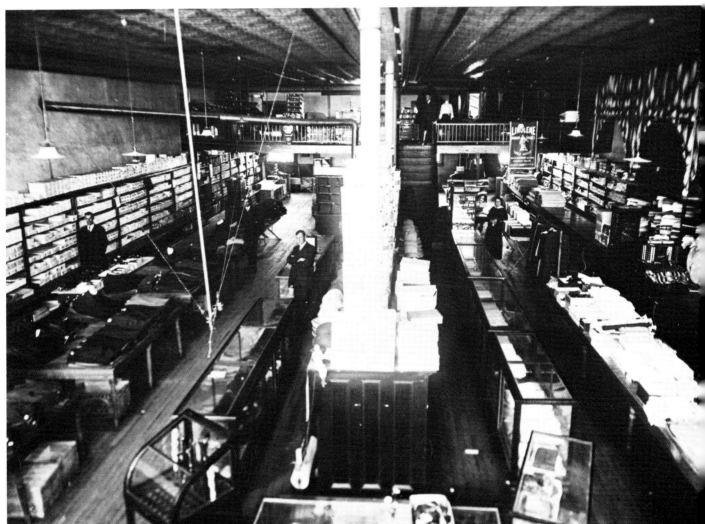

6 Studebaker Buggies
Sold by Spooner HDW Co

Coleman Harness Shop in Norman (top).

McCracken Mitchell Hardware Company in Okmulgee, 1913. Merchandise ranged from baseballs to buggies (middle left).

Studebaker buggies, displayed here in the streets of Hollis, were offered by the Spooner Hardware Company, 1915 (bottom left).

Petty Hardware Store in Hollis (middle right).

Ford Motor Company dealership in Corn, 1927 (bottom right).

109

MANUFACTURING

Cornerstone of Urban Growth

Although the basic wealth of early Oklahoma was land and its bounty, agriculture and natural resources alone could not sustain long-term economic growth or provide steady jobs. The essential building block for such growth was manufacturing, the cornerstone of urban expansion.

From the earliest settlement, even small communities had a few manufacturing operations. Blacksmiths, who spent much of their time shoeing horses and repairing broken implements, also fabricated tools, made wagon wheels, and processed raw materials into finished products. Tinkers, using lasts and leather, set up shops to make shoes and boots for local markets.

The first large-scale industrial development in Oklahoma followed agricultural prosperity. By 1900 virtually every territorial town had a cotton gin where farmers brought their hand-picked produce to have seeds removed and fiber baled. Many towns also had flour mills, where wheat was processed and prepared for market, and grist mills, where corn was ground for feed and meal.

In western Oklahoma the broomcorn boom convinced businessmen to invest in broom factories, where the rough fiber was cleaned, cut, and wrapped into brooms. One of the most unique factories was the macaroni plant in McAlester, where flour was processed into macaroni. Other manufacturing facilities associated with food production were packing plants, ice houses, and bottling works.

Demand, transportation, and raw materials—the foundations of industrial expansion—encouraged a host of other manufacturing enterprises. Brick plants, where clay deposits were fired into bricks and sold to urban developers, appeared in scores of towns. Glass plants, built next to rich deposits of fine sand, responded to periodic construction booms. In the best traditions of free enterprise, each industrial success encouraged successive investment.

From furniture plants to casket factories, manufacturing in early Oklahoma consumed the bounty of the land, created jobs, and attracted financial pioneers needed for leadership in the twentieth century. That success, so important to material progress, preserved Oklahoma's image as the land of opportunity.

111

Blacksmith shop, where wagon wheels and tools were manufactured.

McSpadden Grist and Flour Mill, located on Spring Branch Creek near Tahlequah, 1886 (top left).

Lone Wolf Flour and Grist Mill in Lone Wolf, Oklahoma (bottom left).

112

D.I. Brown's Mill and Store, where customers could buy "Yukon's Best" flour (top right).

Brick plant in Tonkawa, owned by J.H. Conway and S.A. Gindle, where 6 to 20 men could produce 5,000 to 20,000 bricks a day (middle right).

"Contractors and Builders," seen here in Anadarko in 1901, represented one of the most important industries in the territories (bottom right).

113

First blacksmith shop set up on a barren town lot in Guthrie, April, 1889 (top left).

Cunningham Brothers' Blacksmith and Machine Shop in Hollis, 1911 (middle left).

Producing signs for eager merchants was big business in Guthrie, 1889 (bottom left).

114

August Miller's Pioneer Shoe Shop in Norman, 1909 (top right).

Broom factory in western Oklahoma (bottom center).

Ice house, made with blocks of ice cut from a nearby river in Dewey County, 1906 (bottom right).

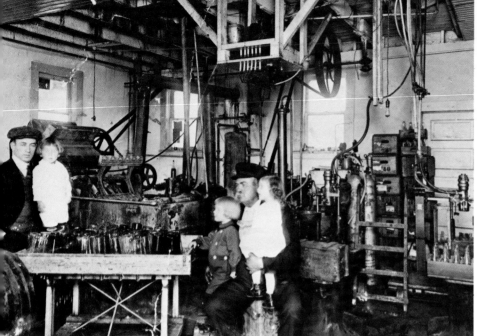

Woodward Bottling Plant, 1906 (top left).

Idabel Coca-Cola bottling plant, 1911 (middle left).

Cord factory in Guthrie (top right).

Cherokee weavers in Tahlequah (middle right).

DeCamp Consolidated Glass Casket Company in Muskogee, 1930 (bottom right center).

McAlester Macaroni Factory, owned by Joe and John Fassino, 1930 (bottom left).

SERVICE

The Legacy
of Main Street

Early day pioneers of Oklahoma were confronted by a host of challenges from court battles to empty stomachs. Some of the problems were matters of life and death; others were simple inconveniences. Regardless of the urgency, most required the services offered along Main Street.

The territorial era was plagued by legal issues as diverse as tribal sovereignty, land contests, and townsite battles, litigation which filled judicial dockets and attracted an army of attorneys. In each case, lawyers were needed to cut through the maze of legal precedents and court procedures.

Set adrift in a sea of unrestricted free enterprise, pioneers also needed financial guidance. Realtors appraised, promoted, and arranged the sale of land, a valuable commodity that represented homes and promise for the future. Bankers safeguarded savings and provided the capital for prosperity and growth.

Meeting the more immediate demands of food and shelter, hotels were built in towns served by railroads or stage lines. Some were grand palaces of brick and stone; others were frame buildings with straw-filled mattresses. Most had restaurants where hungry travelers could order a varied fare, from ham and beans to T-bone steaks, all for a quarter or less.

Also serving the public were communications pioneers such as newspapermen, who promoted the territory and breached the walls of provincial isolation. Other innovative businessmen, stringing telephone lines across the landscape, further reduced isolation and encouraged economic development.

Together with barbers, saloon keepers, photographers, and a host of others, these professionals solved problems, provided comfort, and improved the quality of life for all Oklahomans. Their contributions, from legal protection to home-cooked meals, kept Main Street at the center of life in the territories.

Telephone girl in an unidentified town, a sign of the service economy expanding along Main Street after 1900.

Law office of George M. DeGroff, one of the many attorneys who settled in Guthrie after the land run of 1889 (top left).

Sharing space with a jeweler, this attorney opened his office in Anadarko only days after the land opening of 1901 (top right).

Tent bank, set up in an old corn field, offered financial services to the first settlers of Anadarko, 1901 (middle left).

Researchers at the Sayre Abstract and Title Co., a firm owned by Mrs. A.D. Jones in Sayre, Oklahoma Territory (bottom left).

Two services offered from one building—post office and real estate office in Deltis (middle right).

121

New State Bank, located in Woodward, circa 1900 (bottom right center).

UNITED GROCERY CO. and MARKET

FANCY GROCERIES and GOOD MEATS

"WE SELL FOR LESS"

Hog Enough to want your Business—Man Enough to Appreciate It

UNITED CASH STORES

MENU

Hot Dogs	05
Hamburger	05
Ham Sandwich	10
Chili	10
Soups	10
Ham and Eggs	20
Bacon "	20
Sausage	10
Pork Chops	15
T-Bone Steak	20

BREAKFAST

Hot Cakes	10
Cereals	10
Pie	05
Coffee 5 Milk 2-Glasses	05

Binger Hotel, owned by Mr. and Mrs. A.J. Blankenship, 1904 (top left).

Menu for a Hobart cafe (top center).

Old Arline Hotel in Norman (bottom left).

Commercial Hotel dining room, with food served family style, 1903 (top right).

Chambers Ice Cream Parlor, located on South 2nd Street in Guthrie, 1919 (middle right).

Cafes served everything from pancakes to chicken fried steak, circa 1920 (bottom right).

122

123

Saloon in Lawton, 1902 (top).

Tent barbershop in Anadarko, 1901 (middle left).

John Zimmerman barber shop and pool hall in Tangier, 1906 (bottom left).

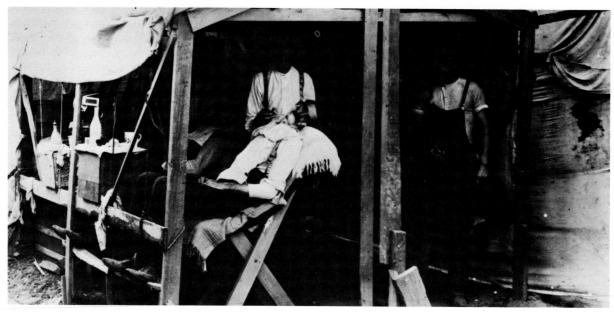

124

John W. Matthews Barber Shop in Guthrie, a social center where a man could get a haircut, shave, and shoe shine *(middle right)*.

Matthews Barber Shop also was a pool hall, a common combination in territorial towns *(bottom right)*.

125

Horse-drawn hearse in Norman *(top left)*.

C.C. Blackwell's cleaning and tailor shop in Prague, 1916 *(bottom left)*.

Funeral procession along a street in El Reno, circa 1905 *(top right)*.

Hollis Laundromat, 1939 *(bottom center)*.

W.E. "Ed" Irwin, famous frontier photographer posed in his Chickasha studio *(bottom right)*.

Hollis Post Office, located in the rear of the old Rist State Bank Building, 1916 (top left).

Reed Post Office, with horse-drawn buggies for town delivery and motorcycles for rural delivery, 1910 (top center).

Hollis Post Office, with letter carriers and officials, 1908 (middle left).

Edgar Sharp, a rural free delivery mail carrier working out of Cooley (bottom left).

128

First telephone lines in Tonkawa, 1902 (top right).

Telegraph "office" at Houck's Tank, located in the Cherokee Outlet before the land run of 1893 (middle right).

First telephone office in Mountain Park, 1914, with operator, Mary Belle Williams (bottom right).

Newstand at the end of Goo-Goo Avenue in Hobart, August 18, 1901 (top left).

Indian print shop, probably at a mission school, 1905 (middle center).

Duncan Banner newspaper office, with hand-set type trays and hand-operated presses (bottom left).

W. E. Showen reading a copy of the Minco Minstrel, 1900 (top right).

Scott Thompson's print shop in Welch (bottom center).

The Woodward Dispatch, with paper boys ready for delivery (bottom right).

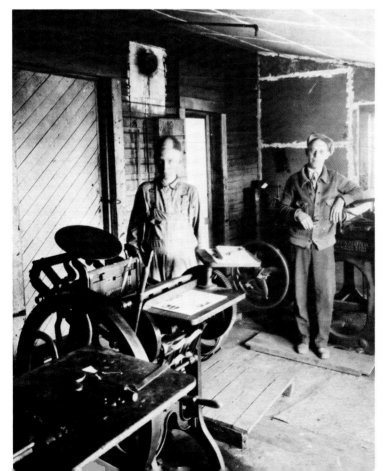

RELIGION

The Freedom
of Choice

Oklahoma has always been a land of freedom, where free people could live, work, and express themselves without fear of oppression. One of the most cherished rights, and one which has added much to the cultural tapestry of our heritage, is freedom of religion.

The first nomadic Indians in Oklahoma brought with them a belief in the "Great Spirit," an omnipresent force which pervaded all things. Good medicine assured victory in battle and in the hunt; bad medicine was a force to be feared.

When the Five Civilized Tribes trekked west, they carried with them a curious blend of Native American religion and Christian beliefs. Missionaries had lived among the tribes since 1801, and after removal devout ministers such as Samuel Worcester and Cyrus Byington established missions in Indian Territory. With the help of tribal leaders such as John Ross and Peter Pitchlynn, they combined schools and religion to educate the heads, hearts, and hands of the Indians.

Non-Indian settlers carried a pantheon of religions into the territories. Greek and Russian immigrants, recruited to work in the mines of the Choctaw Nation, established Greek and Russian Orthodox churches. Blacks, brought in originally as slaves, preserved vestiges of their African cultures. And pioneers, looking for a new chance in the Promised Land, founded Protestant churches, Catholic churches, and Jewish synagogues. All worshiped freely without fear of persecution.

Frontier churches served as both spiritual and social centers of communities. Sunday services were well attended and often continued all day. Tent revivals, conducted by traveling preachers, attracted large crowds and became major events. And the rites of passage, from weddings and baptisms to christenings and funerals, were indivisible elements of church and community life.

Religion in Oklahoma has long represented one of our most treasured institutions—the freedom of choice. That heritage, from Native American beliefs to fundamental Christianity, has added much to the strength of our society.

133

Chief Bacon Rind and other Osage headmen entertain a Cardinal and priest
at the home of Fred Lookout, Pawhuska, 1927.

Zachary Taylor, or "Old Sack", one of the last of the Caddo Peyote leaders (left).

Quapaw, Osage, and Caddo Indians after a Peyote meeting (top right).

Ponca Indians at a Sun Dance, probably held at the 101 Ranch near Ponca City (middle right).

Indian Ghost Dance (bottom right).

135

J.J. Methvin, Methodist missionary to the Kiowas and Comanches, 1894 *(top left)*.

Lillie McKnight and a class at the Cache Creek Mission *(middle left)*.

Bloomfield Seminary, with students and supervisors on their way to a picnic, 1912 *(bottom left)*.

Sacred Heart Benedictine Mission, circa 1900 *(top right)*.

Indian Altar Society at Fairfax, a small town in the old Osage Nation, circa 1920 *(2nd right)*.

136

A.J. Becker, minister at the
Post Oak Mission, baptizing
Winford Asenap, 1938 (3rd
right).

Cherokee Indian Baptist Church
in Eucha, 1943 (bottom right).

Baptism in a creek near Hollis *(top left).*

Wedding couple after the ceremony at a Polish community church *(bottom left).*

Sarah Phillips Wood, reading a Bible at her home *(bottom center).*

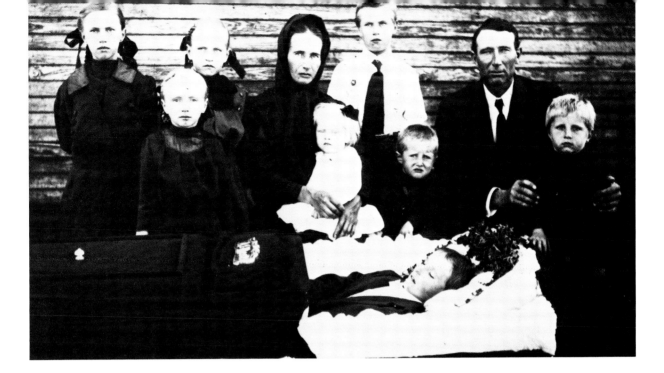

Mourning family grouped around the casket of a 13-year old boy in the Corn community. Such photographs were commonly taken on the frontier *(top right)*.

Mennonites gathered for a funeral procession, 1911 *(middle right)*.

Bible study class at Lesley Church in the Cave Community, just south of Vinson in western Oklahoma *(bottom right)*.

139

Construction of St. Catherine's Catholic Church in Boley, an all black town (top left).

Presbyterian Mission School students and teachers leaving church, 1901 (middle left).

Tent revival, held by E.C. Butler near Shawnee, August, 1911 (bottom left).

Congregation of blacks in Guthrie, seen with Father Placidus Dierick and sisters from St. Joseph's Benedictine Convent (top right).

Congregation of church members in Shawnee (middle right).

Church of Christ tent revival meeting at Hollis, 1910 (bottom right).

142

EDUCATION

A Lamp
in the Darkness

From earliest settlement, Oklahoma was a land of opportunity, a place where hardscrabble pioneers looked to the future with hope. For many, the key to fulfilling that promise was education.

The first schools in Indian Territory were established by missionaries, noble efforts often encouraged by tribal leaders who recognized the benefits of learning. To the missionaries, their schools offered communication with potential converts, the first step in winning not only their souls but also their minds and hands.

Using revenues earned from eastern land sales, tribal leaders opened the first secular schools in the territory. They established district grammar schools and constructed institutions for higher learning, such as the Cherokee Female Seminary and Wheelock Academy. By the Civil War Indian Territory was served by one of the most advanced public school systems in the nation.

The settlers of Oklahoma Territory shared that commitment to education, but without the benefit of public funding. After the land openings, many communities funded grammar schools through subscription and built one-room school houses with donated labor and materials. Teachers, paid $25 a month, usually lived with nearby families during a three-month term.

This respect for education was a dominant theme in the first territorial legislature. During the first session in 1890, legislators funded summer institutes for teachers, established standards for teacher certification, and authorized institutions of higher learning. Thereafter, county, city, and state governments built upon this foundation.

Education, from mission school to graduate school, has contributed much to the tradition of unbounded opportunity in Oklahoma. It is a legacy of accomplishment, of learning, a lamp in the darkness that guides our way into the future.

143

Unidentified one-room school house, the promise of knowledge for many frontier children.

Students going to the dining room at St. Gregory's Abbey, 1901 (top left).

Riverside Indian School, founded in 1871 by Quaker Agents near Anadarko. In 1872 a boarding school for Wichita and Caddo children was constructed (middle left).

Jones Academy, an Indian boys school established in 1891 by the Choctaw Nation (bottom left).

Indian School Cantonment Okla.

Cantonment Indian School, founded in 1897 using buildings abandoned by the military (top right).

Kindergarten class at the Riverside Indian School (middle right).

Nuyaka Boarding School, a mission established in 1882 by Alice Robertson in the Creek Nation (bottom right).

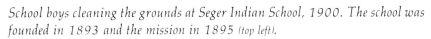

School boys cleaning the grounds at Seger Indian School, 1900. The school was founded in 1893 and the mission in 1895 *(top left)*.

Learning to wash clothes at Riverside Indian School, Anadarko, 1901 *(middle center)*.

Agricultural training at Riverside *(bottom left)*.

Sewing class at Riverside *(top right)*.

Chopping wood at Euchee Mission, established in 1894 with Creek tribal funds. It was located near Sapulpa in the Creek Nation *(bottom right)*.

Sod house that served as the Prairie Center School (top left).

Classroom in early Tonkawa (middle left).

Students preparing for a pageant in Guthrie (bottom left).

Kindergarten students rehearsing a patriotic play (middle left center).

Retrop School, with school wagons, students, and a two-story frame building, 1913 (bottom left center).

Recess at a school in Sapulpa (top right).

Recitation in an early-day school room (bottom right center).

149

Grandview School, February, 1927 (bottom right).

Cherokee teachers' institute held at the Female Seminary near Tahlequah, 1890 (top left).

Students enrolled at Bacone Indian University, 1891 (middle left).

Teachers and helpers at the Cherokee Female Seminary in Tahlequah (bottom left).

Football team at Bacone Indian College, 1903 (top right).

Inaugural procession at the University of Oklahoma, 1925 (bottom right).

151

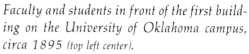

Faculty and students in front of the first building on the University of Oklahoma campus, circa 1895 (top left center).

Old North Tower, constructed in 1896, was the first building on the campus at Central Normal School (Central State University) (middle left).

First building at Southwestern Normal School (Southwestern Oklahoma State University) in Weatherford (bottom left).

Hastings Southwestern Baptist College, located in the western part of Jefferson County, 1907 (top right).

Creek-Seminole College in Boley, an all-black town *(middle right).*

Oklahoma Agricultural and Mechanical College (Oklahoma State University) in Stillwater, 1917 *(bottom right).*

153

Physical Labratory, 1908.
Edmond, Okla.

Office of the Registrar at the University of Oklahoma, 1900 (top left center).

Physical laboratory at Central State Normal School, 1908. Edward Everett Dale, a student at the time, is on the right (middle left).

Chemistry laboratory at the University of Oklahoma (bottom left).

Typing class at Indianola Business College, located in Pittsburg County (top right).

Reading room in the University of Oklahoma library, circa 1920 (bottom right).

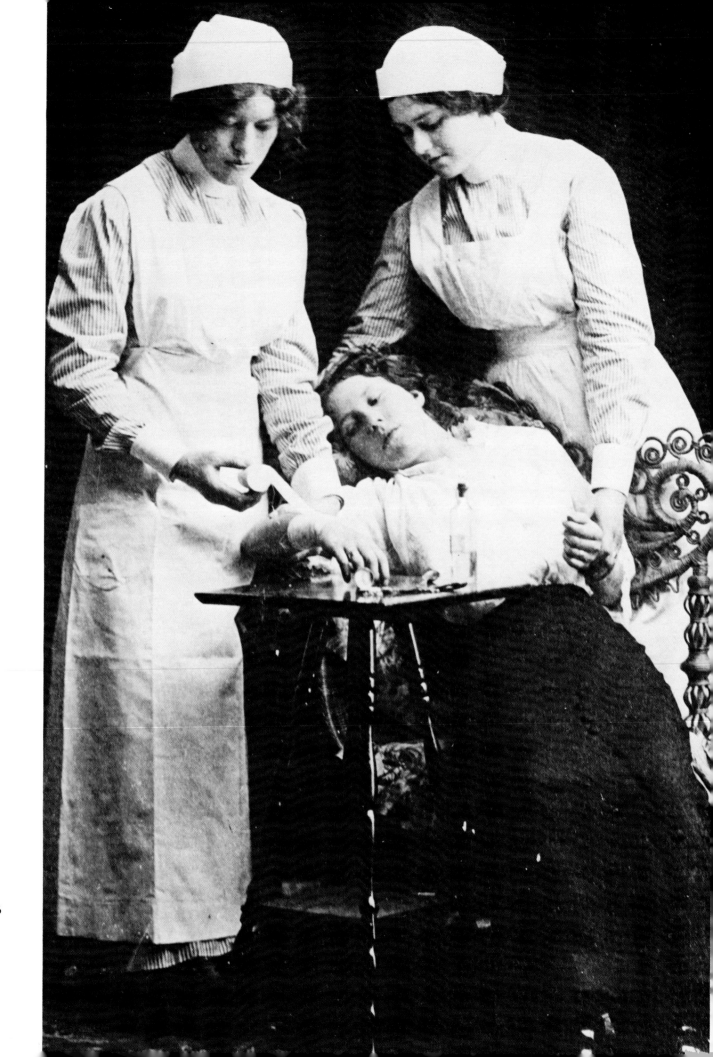

To Heal the Sick and Treat the Injured

To frontier families, doctors, dentists, and nurses were dedicated professionals who treated the sick and healed the injured. Their services, from delivering babies to making dentures, eased the rigors of life in an unforgiving land.

The first physicians in the territory came with explorers to gather data on flora and fauna and treat the sick and injured. They were replaced by doctors assigned to military posts such as Fort Gibson and Fort Towson. Although these physicians were on the frontier primarily to attend soldiers, they usually treated patients from surrounding communities.

Missionaries often doubled as doctors, combining spiritual and temporal healing as they ministered to the Indians. These missionary doctors were joined by Indian physicians who earned medical degrees from Eastern schools.

After the Civil War both government and private physicians came to the territory to serve an increasing population. Because settlements were scattered, many doctors and dentists established circuits with temporary offices in hotels or saloons. Even when they had offices in town, many traveled to their patients' homes in buggies, making their rounds despite the hazards of travel and weather.

Health care in Oklahoma advanced rapidly after these rugged beginnings. Private and public hospitals were opened with the most advanced care. Medical, dental, and nursing schools were established to train needed professionals. And research centers were funded to develop new treatments and expand knowledge. Each contributed to the effectiveness of health care.

From little black bags to neuro-surgery, medical care in Oklahoma has improved during the past century. That progress, made possible by the early achievements of pioneer doctors, dentists, and nurses, is a true testament to hard work and training.

157

Nurses, who cared for everything from scratches to the vapors.

Family doctor and his faithful horse ready to make their rounds in the "buckboard days" of medical care (top left).

Early day medicine show poster (bottom left).

Automobiles made house calls quicker and more effective (top right).

Central State Hospital, built in Norman in 1897, was originally called the Oklahoma Sanitarium (bottom center).

Sanitarium in Sulphur, circa 1910 (bottom right).

158

FREE SHOW!

DON'T MISS IT.—TO-NIGHT!

THE
Oregon
Indian Medicine
Company

Visits your town for the purpose of introducing to your notice its medicines. To attract attention they will give a series of

HIGH CLASS MORAL ENTERTAINMENTS.

Which will amuse you, while they will endeavor to enlighten you to the fact that their remedies are something of great importance to many people.

OREGON INDIAN MEDICINE CO'S. UAPARALLELD ADVERTISING METEO

A Refined, Marvelous, Unique, Moral Entertainment.

COMEDY CONCERT CO

THE WORLD MOVES, WE KEEP UP

We Are In The Race!   We Set The Pace!   We Go Ahead!

We employ the Best Singers, Musicians, Actors and Comedians. Some are Negro Delineators, others Irish, and some Dutch.

IT WILL SURELY DO YOU GOOD TO GO.

THE SINGING IS SUPERB!
MUSIC ENCHANTING!
COMEDIES CONVULSING!
FARCES UPROARIOUS!

This is One of Our Best Shows,
Under a Model Manag..

WE TEACH
Virtue, Morality and Health.

WHO IS THIS MAN?
He Is Donald McKay,
The Greatest in His Class.

His record at the War Department Washington, D. C., stands higher than any other government scout or Indian fighter, living or dead. He gave to civilization Indian Medicines, that many charlatans and impostors have tried to imitate. You will have The Genuine Medicines Introduced by this Company

YOU CAN COME AND SEE US
Make Cripples Walk, the Deaf to Hear, and Make Sick People Well.

Th Entertainments given by the
OREGON INDIAN MEDICINE CO.
Are not to be confounded or classed with any other so-called Indian Medicine company.

Their Reputation and Responsibilities are Too Great.

WE ARE THE ORIGINAL AND ONLY GENUINE INDIAN MEDICINE CO. in existence. Our medicines were actually derived from the Indians. No other so-called Indian Medicine Co. can claim what we can prove. We Prove It in order to Protect Our Rights. Read our other books, pamphlets, guides and circulars that will be distributed to all visitors at our entertainments.

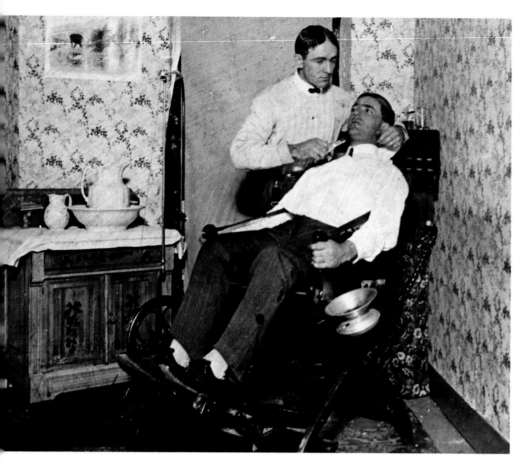

Dentist office in Stillwater, 1902 (top left).

Dr. R.J. Pendleton and his dental office, circa 1900 (bottom left).

Dr. Lucille Blachley in her Norman office, circa 1920 (top center).

Annual back-to-school visit to the doctor (top right).

Dr. E.C. Williams in his optometrist's office in Woodward, 1917 (bottom right).

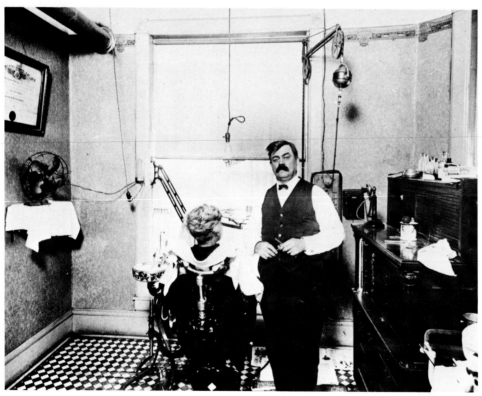

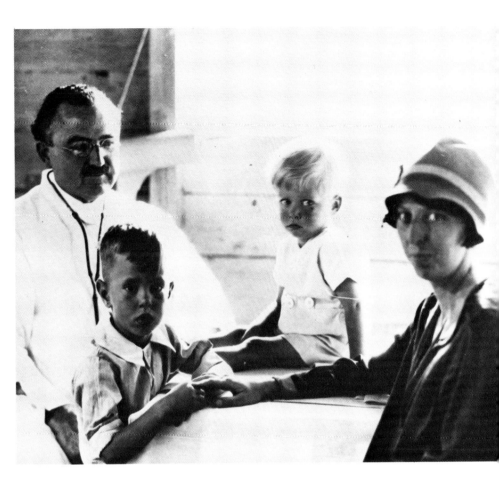

161

Early X-ray equipment in Dr. Alexander Barkley's office in Hobart, 1916 (top left).

Medical students in an early anatomy class (bottom left).

Student body at the Epworth College of Medicine, 1909. Two years later the school became the University of Oklahoma School of Medicine (top right).

Medical students and staff gathered to observe surgery (bottom right).

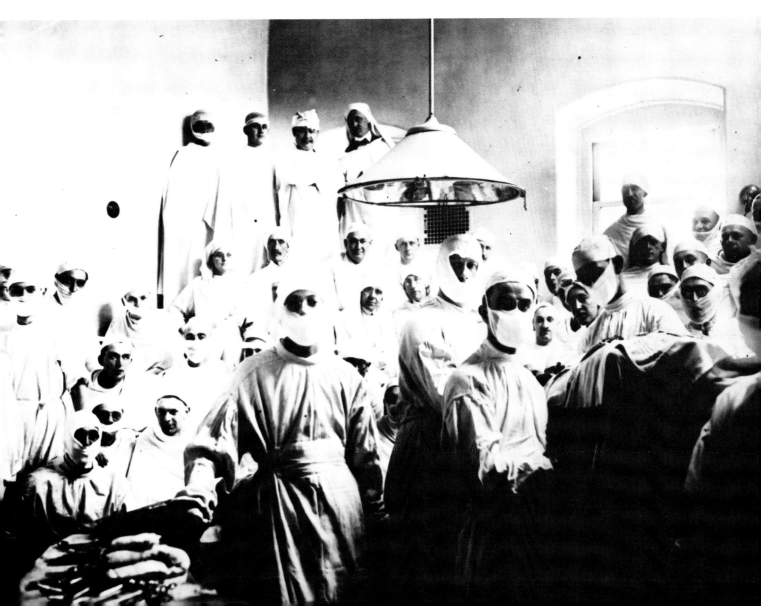

RELAXATION

The Pursuit
of Happiness

Oklahomans are generally hard-working people, willing to toil long hours in field and office. This dedication to work, however, is tempered by the pursuit of leisure—the attempt to get away from it all. From picnics on the prairie to weekends at the lake, relaxation has been an important part of our heritage.

On the frontier, settlers occasionally escaped their labors to enjoy the fruits of the new land. They attended socials and box suppers at local schools. And with friends and family, they held picnics with baskets of fried chicken, homemade pies, and canned preserves.

Men organized hunting and fishing trips, with extended forays into the field. Fellowship around the campfire and the thrill of the hunt offered security and emotional release from the pressures of daily life, as well as meat for the table. Many found similar fellowship at domino parlors, pool halls, or saloons.

Women formed sewing, social, and service clubs for the same reasons. They gathered to share information, learn from one another, and bask in the glow of friendship. Many also found satisfaction in helping their community through concerted action in clubs. Whatever the reasons, the fellowship offered respite from daily chores.

Sites for recreation abounded in the new land. Rivers, such as the Illinois, the Deep Fork, and the Kiamichi encouraged fishing, boating, and swimming. Beauty spots, such as Turner Falls, Medicine Park, and the Great Salt Plain attracted campers and sightseers. In the twentieth century, man-made lakes such as Tenkiller, Grand, and Texoma expanded the possibilities and made pleasure boating and swimming available to a leisure-conscious public.

The pursuit of relaxation has been an important aspect of life in Oklahoma, a reward for labor, diligence, and achievement. From social clubs to campouts, opportunities for leisure have abounded.

165

Watermelon feast after a wedding, held at Red Rock Canyon near Hinton, 1906.

Hunters, led by an Indian guide, on the Caddo Reservation near Chickasha, 1899 (top left).

Early day camp wagon used for temporary living quarters in the field (middle left).

Picnic party in the Navajo Mountains, circa 1895 (bottom left).

Building a barbeque pit for a Fourth of July celebration, 1900 (top right).

Picnic lunch before a baseball game in Southwest Oklahoma (middle right).

A family outing near Chelsea, 1920 (bottom right).

Turner Falls, a famous landmark in the Arbuckle Mountains, circa 1900 (top left).

Boating on the Arkansas River in a flat-bottom boat, 1895 (top center).

Tourists on a resort bus at Medicine Park, 1919 (middle center).

Miami Tourist Park, located on Route 66, offered tents, pavilions, and electricity for an increasingly mobile public in the 1920s (bottom left).

Cane pole fishing in rivers was popular recreation in the territory (top right).

Bathing beaches, usually man-made swimming holes, were popular social spots from the 1900s to the 1950s (bottom center).

Sailing on Lake Altus, known as Lugert Lake when constructed in the 1930s (bottom right).

169

Members of the Womens' Christian Temperance Union at Knowles, 1916 *(top left)*.

The Royal Neighbors Lodge at Hollis, circa 1910 *(bottom left)*.   Sewing club at Mehan, 1901 *(top right)*.

Elmore City members of the Woodmen of the World, a fraternal organization popular across the nation, 1916 *(bottom center)*.

Members of the Sokol, a Polish fraternal order in Prague, 1906 *(bottom right)*.

Saloon in Oklahoma Territory *(top left)*.

Polish men celebrating the Fourth of July in Harrah, 1920 *(bottom left)*.

Craps, although illegal, was a common game in most towns of the territory at the turn of the century *(top right)*.

"Spit and whittle club." *(middle right)*.

Checkers, the great board game enjoyed by all ages *(bottom right)*.

173

174

Expressions of the Human Spirit

Life on the frontier was rich in music, dance, and drama, forms of entertainment which echoed the emotions of a new land. This tradition of personal and professional achievement, so important to cultural development, provided a foundation of creativity that enriched the minds and hearts of Oklahomans.

Music and dance probably were brought into the region by nomadic Indians who sang praises to the Great Spirit. Their descendants, the Five Civilized and Southern Plains tribes, carried those early forms of expression to full achievement with dances and songs for every occasion and need.

Pioneers brought with them a rich legacy of artistic expression. In boomer camps, ever-present musicians sawed on their fiddles while hopeful settlers danced. On the range, cowboys sang to entertain themselves and calm their cattle. In isolated sod houses, pioneer women played tunes on treasured pump organs brought west over the rocky roads of migration.

In one-room schoolhouses students produced plays and Christmas shows, events which drew large crowds. Traveling entertainers, using rented halls with candle-lit stages, performed productions from New York and London. And in scattered churches, choir members sang praises to Him, expressing appreciation for blessings and hope for the future.

Oklahoma was fertile soil for professional entertainment, a quality proven by the flamboyance of the Wild West shows. Organized by frontier promoters and pioneers such as the Miller Brothers and Gordon "Pawnee Bill" Lillie, these shows combined images of the Wild West with circus performances to create a unique form of entertainment.

That spirit of artistic expression can still be found in community theaters, school bands, and dance classes. It is a tradition of excellence, of personal expression and aesthetic appreciation that reflects the world around us. The images of that heritage, from class plays to symphony orchestras, can tell us much about ourselves.

175

Reading about the coming attractions of the 101 Ranch Wild West Show, a unique band of entertainers based on a ranch just outside of Ponca City.

176

Touring actors in Oklahoma City, 1893 *(top left)*.

Musician with sheet music, piano, and guitar *(bottom left)*.

Vaudeville poster, advertising coming attractions *(top center)*.

The Club Theater in Guthrie, which erected this stage in a tent, 1889 *(top right)*.

Cast of "Three Old Maids," a play performed in Oklahoma City, 1892 *(bottom right)*.

177

Minstrel show staged by the Pauls Valley Lions Club, 1950 (top left).

Play rehearsal at an Oklahoma City school, 1896. (bottom left).

Cast of an elementary school production of "Cinderella," 1908 (top right).

Members of the Tulsa Civic Ballet, circa 1968 (bottom right).

178

Indian ribbon dance performed near Okemah in the old Creek Nation *(top left)*.

Fiddlers and dancers in a prairie community *(bottom left)*.

Man and his fiddle, the promise of song and dance *(top right).*

Square dancing to a band and caller, circa 1955 *(middle right).*

Exhibition of Mexican folk dances at the Oklahoma State Fair, circa 1960 *(bottom right).*

The University of Oklahoma Mandolin Club, 1900 (top left).

Musicians with a variety of stringed instruments available at a Hennessey store, 1904 (bottom left).

Western Swing Band of Johnnie Lee Wills, long time feature at Cain's Ball Room in Tulsa (top right).

Friars at St. Gregory's Abbey assembled for band practice, 1898 (middle right).

Jimmie Wilson and the Catfish String Band, a regular feature on KVOO Radio in Tulsa (bottom right).

183

Charlie Christian, outstanding jazz guitarist who got his start in Oklahoma City *(top center)*.

Woody Guthrie, American folk hero and song writer born in Okemah *(middle left)*.

Joseph Benton, Oklahoma tenor who achieved fame on the stages of Europe *(middle center)*.

The Blue Devils, a regionally famous jazz band based in Oklahoma City during the 1920s and 1930s (top right).

Oklahoma City Symphony Orchestra, 1949 (bottom).

1926 OFFICIAL ROUTE 1926

MILLER BROS
101 RANCH
REAL WILD WEST
AND
GREAT FAR EAST-
HEADQUARTERS
MARLAND OKLA

No. 23

Date	City	Railroad	Miles
TWENTY-SIXTH WEEK			
Oct. 18th	Oklahoma City, Okla.	Frisco	41
" 19	Sapulpa, Okla.	Frisco Ry.	104
" 20	Henryetta, Okla.	Frisco Ry.	45
" 21	Muskogee, Okla.	Frisco Ry.	52
" 22	Fort Smith, Ark.	Frisco Ry.	167
" 23	Hugo, Okla.	Frisco Ry.	143
TWENTY-SEVENTH WEEK			
Oct. 25th	Paris, Texas,	Frisco Ry.	25
" 26th	Greenville, Tex.	T. M. Ry.	52
" 27th	Texakana, Ark.	Cotton Belt Ry.	132
" 28th	Hope, Ark.	M. P. Ry.	32
" 29th	El Dorado, Ark.	M. P. Ry.	88
" 30th	Monroe, La.	M. P. Ry.	89
" 31st	Vidalia, La. (Mat. only)	M. P. Ry.	113

"TEX" COOPER, Mail Agent

WORKING BOY TICKET

MILLER BROTHERS
101 RANCH
REAL WILD WEST
AND
GREAT FAR EAST-
SHOWS
GENERAL OFFICES AND
WINTER QUARTERS
MARLAND, OKLA.

ADMIT ONE WORKING BOY
GOOD ONLY FOR BOY WHO WORKED
VOID IF SOLD

Route schedule for the 101 Ranch Show in the fall of 1926 *(top left)*.

A ticket given to boys who helped set up for a performance of the 101 Ranch Wild West Show *(bottom left)*.

Loading show horses at the 101 Ranch *(top right)*.

Horse-drawn calliope in the opening parade through town *(bottom right)*.

Movie set on the Miller Brothers 101 Ranch (top left).

Scrip redeemable at the 101 Ranch Store (middle left).

Performance day at the 101 Ranch (bottom left).

Patrons gather to buy tickets for the big show (top center).

Clown and his mule in the 101 Show (bottom center).

Poster which announced the coming attraction (right).

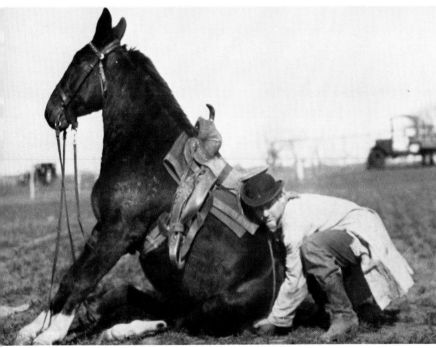

Program for Pawnee Bill's Pioneer Days Wild West Show (top left).

Pawnee Bill's "Wild West and Great Far East" museum (top center).

Fox Hastings, a famous bulldogger in the wild west shows (bottom left).

Indians were a popular feature in the elaborately staged shows *(top right)*.

Wild broncs and cowboys—images of entertainment that reflected the passing frontier *(bottom right)*.

191

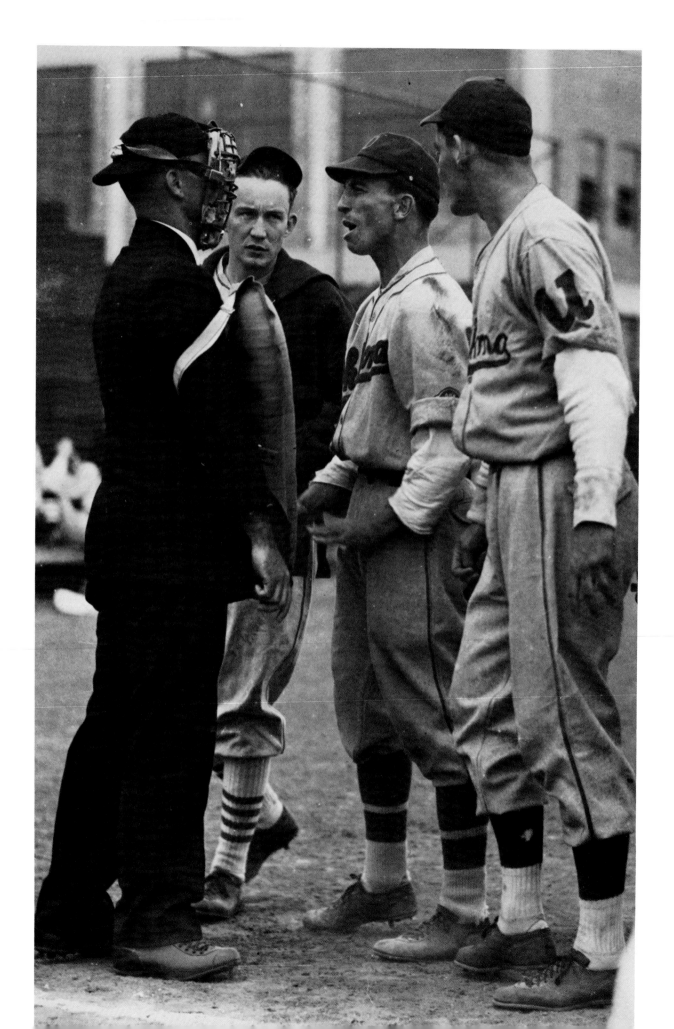

CELEBRATIONS AND SPORTS

For the Fun of It

Oklahomans have always encouraged celebrations and sports, whether by gathering at a feast to commemorate a battle or attending a baseball game to win a title. This motivation—to celebrate, to compete, to have fun—has contributed much to the cultural and social variety of life.

Both Southern Plains and Woodland Indians developed games and celebrations. Many tribes played a form of stick ball, an aggressive sport with a large field and unlimited numbers of players. Most Indians also were enthusiastic horsemen, racing their mounts to test muscle and skill. All celebrated with feasts and dancing to commemorate important events, from raids and hunts to guests and marriages.

Pioneers matched that ability to mark the mileposts of life. They recognized traditional holidays such as Thanksgiving, Christmas, and the Fourth of July, and added others such as '89er Day, Statehood Day, and Decoration Day. The opportunities increased with observances of birthdays, marriages, graduations, and reunions. All justified a celebration.

Entire communities shared in many of these events. Parades stretched for blocks with homemade floats, marching bands, and horsemen. Fairs in every county and town attracted celebrants to agricultural displays, cooking contests, side shows, horse races, and amusements. Other well-attended celebrations included pow-wows, May Day festivities, and bandstand concerts.

Sports attracted equally large crowds. Baseball teams, organized anywhere nine players could be found, challenged neighboring communities to high-spirited games that turned into all-day events with picnics and parties. High schools and colleges also sponsored team sports, from basketball and football to tennis and boxing. Each contest was anticipated with glee and played with enthusiasm.

Whether it was a boisterous parade or a set of tennis, sports and celebrations promoted community traditions, team effort, and healthy competition—qualities that bound people together as they expressed the joy of living.

193

The traditional confrontation, umpire and manager, at a University of Oklahoma baseball game, 1944.

Shaff's marching band in a Tonkawa parade, 1900 (top left).

Float in the Fourth of July parade in Norman, 1901 (2nd left).

Parade in Mutual celebrating the first anniversary of statehood, 1908 (3rd left).

Waurika Booster Band, ready for a parade down Main Street (bottom left).

St. Patrick's Day parade down the streets of Shamrock (top right).

"Miss Liberty" and "Uncle Sam" riding in a Fourth of July parade during World War I (bottom right).

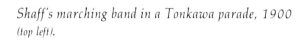

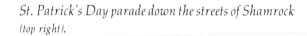

194

Raffles such as this one in Woodward were events that brought the entire town out into the streets *(top left)*.

Outdoor political rally in Lexington, 1889. Politicians were good entertainment in the years before mass communication *(middle left)*.

Political speech by Lee Cruce, Oklahoma's second governor, 1910 *(bottom left)*.

Anadarko's first anniversary celebration, 1902 *(top right)*.

Statehood celebration in Hollis, 1907 *(bottom right)*.

Corn Carnival in Minco,
1908 (top left).

Cheyenne-Arapaho Indian
Fair at Watonga, 1912
(middle left).

Comanche dancers at Cra-
terville Park, a rodeo
grounds and race track near
Cache in the Wichita
Mountains, circa 1920
(bottom left).

Display of vegetables at the first Roger Mills County Fair (top right).

Livestock judging at the Jackson County Fair in Altus, 1941 (middle right).

Warren 4-H Club with their exhibit at the Jackson County Fair, 1941 (bottom right).

199

First motion picture house in Ponca City (top).

May Day and the Maypole dance was a popular celebration each spring (2nd left).

Norman Volunteer Fire Department, prepared for a Fourth of July parade (3rd left).

Street fair in Sentinel, complete with exhibit tents, bands, and amusement rides (bottom left).

Troupe of trapeze artists who performed at the University of Oklahoma in 1900 *(middle center)*.

Rollercoaster at Hyde Park, 1910 *(middle right)*.

Halloween party, always one of the most colorful celebrations of the year *(bottom right)*.

Girl's basketball at the Oklahoma Agricultural and Mechanical College, circa 1900 *(top left)*.

Tennis on the court by the old East Side School in Norman *(top center)*.   Horse racing in Tonkawa *(bottom left)*.

Miss Maude DeCou, librarian, and Mrs. Grace King Maguire, music teacher, posed with their bicycles in Norman *(top right)*.

Track and field competition at the University of Oklahoma *(bottom right)*.

204

Jim Thorpe, the Sac and Fox Indian from Oklahoma who became an Olympic star and the world's greatest football player (top left).

Winner of Woodward's first 200-mile automobile race, April 21, 1916. Time was 4 hours, 13 minutes, and 54 seconds (bottom left).

Football teams of the University of Oklahoma and Arkansas City do battle on the field, 1898 (top right).

University of Oklahoma football player carries the ball through the Iowa State line, circa 1920 (middle right).

Boxing match at Fort Sill, near Lawton (bottom center).

Starting four for the University of Oklahoma polo team (bottom right).

CHILDREN

Growing Up in Oklahoma

Children represent Oklahoma's most important resource. They embody the future with all the hope and promise of tomorrow. They encourage the hard work and persistence needed to build a better world. But most importantly, they represent the love and strength of families binding one generation to the next.

Growing up in Oklahoma has been an exciting education for most young people, even when times were hard. Children of Southern Plains Indians learned the lessons of trail life with its constant movement and few comforts. By playing games, they learned to use weapons and track game. By helping with camp activities, they learned to prepare food and process hides. By listening to tribal tales around the campfire, they learned the traditions of their people. All prepared them for the future.

Although from a different culture, non-Indian children learned similar lessons. Games such as shinny and kick-the-can developed muscles and taught them how to get along with neighbors. Chores such as churning butter, feeding the chickens, and handling livestock taught them the values of work. And listening to scriptures and stories around the fireplace taught them the moral, social, and spiritual traditions of their forefathers. Each was another step toward maturity.

Outside the home children found an inviting world with unlimited possibilities. During hot summer months creeks became swimming holes and fishing spots. Winter snow encouraged sledding, skating, and snowball fights. Stacked logs became forts, mud puddles became lakes, and sticks became guns. Every season, rain or shine, the land yielded to the imaginations of youth.

From childhood games to doing chores, growing up in early Oklahoma offered many choices. The values inherited, the lessons learned prepared them for the challenges and opportunities ahead.

Unidentified boy, whose uniform and pose reflected the world around him, circa 1918.

Indian students at Cache Creek Mission, west of Apache (top left).

Children playing at Cache Creek Mission, learning skills that would prepare them for the future (middle left).

Indian children from St. Patrick's Mission in a Fourth of July parade, Anadarko, 1910 (top right).

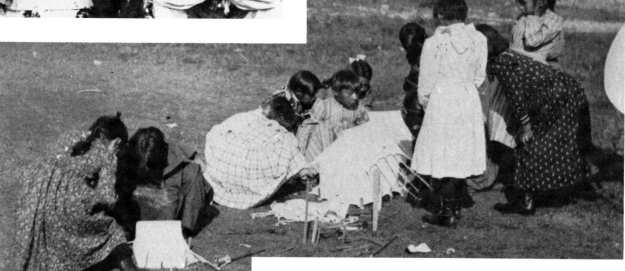

Father Isidore Ricklin, with a few of his students at St. Gregory's Abbey, 1919 (bottom center).

Christmas time at an Episcopal chapel (bottom right).

Young child, dressed in best clothing, was the pride of her father *(top left)*.

Photographed at Anadarko, these children were playing with a toy cradle board and doll, encouraging the continuation of tribal traditions *(bottom left)*.

Cheyenne family, the Sweet-Waters, in 1900 *(top center)*.

Kiowa youngster with his Christmas gifts from the Episcopal Mission Chapel *(bottom center)*.

Traditions of child rearing, such as carrying babies on the mother's back, transcended changing life styles (right).

Children and horses, a common sight in early Oklahoma *(top left)*.

Young cowboy, with oversize hat and boots, astride a calf at the 101 Ranch *(bottom left)*.

Farm animals often served as unwilling playmates *(bottom center)*.

Bouncing baby boy in a little black bag, a unique pose that undoubtedly pleased proud parents (top center).

Youngsters with their dog, a universal image of inseparable friends (middle right).

Cane poles and fishing holes, both challenge and entertainment (bottom right).

213

Jacob Buffalo Thigh, son of Buffalo Thigh, dressed in incongruous cowboy garb (top left).

Indian children in traditional dress, from beaded breast plate to hand-tooled moccasins (bottom left).

Osage children, 1913 (bottom center).

Kiowa women and their babies *(top right)*.

Proud Pawnee family, with their baby strapped into a decorative cradle board *(bottom right)*.

215

Young girl and her prized possessions (top left).

Cousins Jennie and Charles Fassino, McAlester, 1907 (bottom left).

Young girl with her doll and baby buggie (bottom center).

Sharecropper family suffering the devastation of the Great Depression, circa 1934 (top right).

Boy and his bicycle, a universal image of youth (middle right).

Young business people, learning the challenges of the marketplace, circa 1930 (bottom right).

Sisters, facing the world together, developed bonds that would withstand the passing of years (top left).

Snow, sleds, and children, a compensation for winter weather (bottom left).

Wash tub full of baby (top center).

Children with fruits of the family garden (top right).

Youngsters with stick horses and homemade toys were limited only by their fertile imaginations (bottom right).

The Drummond children of Hominy, dressed in their best clothes (top left).

Three generations of Oklahomans in Sapulpa, circa 1920 (bottom left).

Baby with her great-grandmother, the wisdom of the past and the promise of the future (top right).

Clara Shuck and her daughter, Ruth, 1906 (middle right).

Christmas with the family, an image of love and togetherness (bottom right).

Photo Credits

Most of the photographs in this publication come from the Western History Collections, University of Oklahoma Library. The following individuals and organizations donated photographs to these collections:

Armantrout Studios Collection, J. A. Baker, Dr. T. L. Ballenger, Dr. Alexander Barkley, Dr. A. J. Becker, R. S. Bedford, Page Belcher, Joseph Benton, Dr. Lucille Blachley, W. W. Blackburn;

D. R. Boyd, W. S. Bruner, Bureau of Land Management Collection, W. H. Butcher, W. S. Campbell, George Case, Muriel Chew, Frank Clements, C. W. Cole;

E. A. Coleman, Emma Coleman, Jim Collon, William J. Connor, Corn Historical Society Collection, Kenneth Crook, Dillon Cunningham, Robert E. Cunningham, E. E. Dale;

E. E. Darnell, Deal Studio Collection, S. J. Deason, DeCamp Consolidated Glass Casket Co. Collection, Ada Depenbrink, Sam DeVenney, Dewey County Public Library Collection, Dewey Public Library Collection, Vince Dillon, Division of Manuscripts Collection;

John Dunn, John F. Easley, Farm Security Administration Collection, Walter Ferguson, A. A. Forbes, General Personalities Collection, Armand Gibson, Mrs. M. J. Gould, S. R. Hadsell, E. B. Hamilton;

Jay Hargett, Walter M. Harrison, Edna Hatfield, Roy E. Heffner, Hurley L. Henderson, Al Herring, Dr. A. G. Hirshfield, Don L. Hofsommer, Hollis Public Library Collection, William Hollis;

Howard Studios Collection, Waddie Hudson, Patrick Hurley, Rollin Hutchins, Irwin Brothers, Louise James, A. D. Jones, Kali-Inla Collection, George Killingsworth, Kiowa County Historical Society Collection;

E. R. Kraettli, Emil Lenders, George Levite, P. K. Lewis, Liberty National Bank Collection, Mary Louise Ligon, G. W. Lillie, George Long, Magnolia Petroleum Company Collection, McAlester Public Library Collection;

W. C. McClure, McCurtain County Historical Society Collection, Medicine Show Collection, Miller Bros. 101 Ranch Collection, Moore Public Library Collection, J. W. Morris, William Munger, Joseph Murphy, Norman Public Library Collection, C. A. Northstein;

Oklahoma Geological Survey Collection, Oklahoma Semi-Centennial Collection, Oklahoma State Dental Association Collection, Okmulgee County Boosters Collection, C. C. Paine, Mrs. G. C. Paine, Frank Parman, J. D. Pate, W. L. Payne, Dr. R. J. Pendleton;

Amy Perkins, Mrs. J. T. Perkins, Frank Phillips, Clyde C. Pickard, Poster Collection, W. S. Prettyman, J. L. Rader, W. B. Randall, Grace Ray, Charles Richard;

Robbins Collection, Glenn Sansing, William Scherman, Mrs. William, A. M. Seran, Shawnee Public Library Collection, W. E. Showen, J. A. Shuck, M. R. Shumard, George Sohlberg;

Don Sporleder, St. Gregory's Abbey Collection, M. C. Stephens, A. P. Swearingen, Dr. G. W. Taylor, W. E. Tomlinson, Tonkawa Public Library Collection, University of Oklahoma Class of 1906 Collection, D. C. Ward, Fred L. Wenner, Lida White, A. J. Williams, John Windolph, and Woodward County Collection.

Other photographs in this publication appear courtesy of the following individuals and organizations. The position of each photograph is described by page number and location on the page (t-top, c-center, b-bottom, r-right, l-left):

Brenda Anderson, 126-127bc; Alice Brown, 115br; Kenny Brown, 116bl; Mrs. L. Chambers, 123c; Alberta Cunningham, 128tl; Marie Davis, 138t; Mrs. Esther Decker, 49t; Madge Dombrowski, 93t; Earnest Edwards, 52b, 100t; Ernest Edwards, 51t, 131bl;

Earl England, 28b; Ralph Enix, 101t, 102t, 103b; Ethel Fariss, 50t; Georgia Fariss, 97t; Mrs. Charles Fassino, 216bl, 217lc; Jim Flood, 92t; Mrs. Ollie Fried, 125c, b; Ed Fulmer, 116c; Mrs. Ora Groves, 109c, 170b;

Mrs. Chester Harmon, 139b; Sally Helms, 141c; Mrs. Lizzie Jezek, 171bl; Kerr-McGee, 82tr, tl, b, 83t, bl; Guy Logsdon, 62-63b, 183b, c, 184tr, lc, 185t; Mattie McDaniel, 96b; McFarlin Library, University of Tulsa, Sinclair Collection, 66, 68t, 72c, 73t, 75c, t, 77b, 80t; Mrs. James McKay, 171t; Mrs. Leo McKee, 148bl; Pete Meget, 139t;

Museum of the Great Plains, 176b, 180b; Oklahoma Historical Society, 14tc, 16tl, tr, bc, 17tl, tr, 18c, 19t, c, b, 21t, c, 40t, 74c, 77t, 83br, 145c, 153c, 168tl, 202tl; Drummond Home, 220t; Kathryn Outlaw, 36; Roger Pritchett, 126b; Mrs. Charles Richard, 155t; Lena Rollins, 108b; Joe Sheriff, 128lc; *Sooner Catholic Magazine*, 132, 137tc, 140t, 141t, 209t; Stephens County Historical Museum, 106b, 110;

Bill Unger, 109b; United States Navy, Office of Naval History, 20t; Arnold Wedel, 139c; Henry Wiebe, 149rc; Elenora Wyskup, 138bl, 172b; Ceola Youngblood, 140b; and Mrs. Stanley Yousey, 34b

Index

226